THE DOLMEN PRESS

A Celebration

THE DOLMEN PRESS

A Celebration

Edited by Maurice Harmon

THE LILLIPUT PRESS
DUBLIN

First published 2001 by
THE LILLIPUT PRESS LTD
62–63 Sitric Road, Arbour Hill,
Dublin 7, Ireland
www.lilliputpress.ie

A CIP record for this title is available from
The British Library.

1 3 5 7 9 10 8 6 4 2

ISBN 1 901866 75 0 (HBK)
ISBN 1 901866 76 9 (LTD ED.)

*The Lilliput Press receives financial assistance
from An Chomhairle Ealaíon / The Arts Council of Ireland.*

Designed by Raymond Gunn and set in Palatino by
Redsetter Ltd, Dublin
Printed by ColourBooks, Baldoyle, Dublin

CONTENTS

ILLUSTRATIONS

THE DOLMEN PRESS

A Celebration

INTRODUCTION

Fifty years after its founding, the Dolmen Press and its founder Liam Miller are still associated with the publication of beautiful books and with the fresh stirrings that took place in Irish literature in the early years of the 1950s. The new generation of writers emerging from the fallow years of the forties were fortunate in finding a publisher committed to the idea of providing an outlet for their work in Ireland itself, thereby releasing them from the uncertain prospects of finding a publisher in London. Furthermore, Miller believed in the idea of a sustained, mutually satisfying relationship between the writer and the publisher. The kind of co-operation that had characterized the making of plays in the early years of the Abbey Theatre was replicated in the way that he and the poets worked together. Many who published a book with Dolmen had the rare experience of collaborating with a skilled and imaginative craftsman seeking to match design, materials and literary content.

The value of this principle may be seen in the careers of Thomas Kinsella and John Montague, whose work he encouraged from the beginning and who in turn valued the dedication, energy and imagination he brought to the publication of their successive collections. Each work was considered on its individual terms; for each Miller sought an appropriate format. For the first time an Irish writer could have what Kinsella describes as a 'professional primary publisher in Ireland'.

The effect of this stability and continuity may be seen also in the later career of Austin Clarke. Miller provided an outlet for the poet's unexpected late revival, was loyal to him up to his death in 1974 and published his posthumous work. A poet who had been bringing out his own work in limited private editions was presented more widely as a significant figure by the prestigious Dolmen.

The highest achievement of the Dolmen ethos came in the production of Thomas Kinsella's translation of *The Táin* in 1969. In Miller's view this work alone, a folio of three hundred pages set in fourteen-point Perpetua type with Felix Titling display characters and with one hundred and thirty brush drawings by Louis le Brocquy, justified the existence of the Press. Both le Brocquy and Kinsella pay warm and grateful tribute herein to his achievement in this enterprise. A similar spirit of co-operation and excitement attended the 1972 production of John Montague's *The Rough Field,* in which, as Thomas Dillon Redshaw points out,

Miller successfully adapted the woodcuts of the Elizabethan artist John Derricke to illustrate Montague's historical meditation on his Ulster background.

The Dolmen Press fostered talent and educated taste. The strength of the Press, Rory Brennan writes, 'lay in its flair, in a kind of celebratory élan, in being a crucible, a vessel, an inspiring means'. It was also important to the development of Irish literary studies. Those who wanted to discover what was new in Irish writing could rely to a significant degree on Dolmen's publication lists. When it made its first (and, as it turned out, only) appearance in 1962, *The Dolmen Miscellany*, containing work by a rising generation of Irish writers, was a signpost to what was happening. And as collection after collection appeared — by Thomas Kinsella, John Montague, Richard Murphy — those who appreciated fine poetry and fine books quickly realized the worth of the Dolmen imprint.

When Liam Miller published *Dolmen XXV*, a descriptive and illustrated bibliography to commemorate the twenty-fifth anniversary of Dolmen's founding, it was evident that the Press had made a significant contribution to Irish culture. In the introduction Miller recalls the innocent early years, the 'execrable' presswork and survival 'entirely due to the qualities of the writers we tried to serve'. 'Bonds so formed', he writes, remembering the writers who set up their own work, cut large sheets with a kitchen knife, folded inky sheets and distributed type back into the cases, 'are not lightly severed and, looking back over the work of all those years — a couple of shelves of mostly slim volumes — I can discern a certain order and progression in the work of our press and in the loyalties that went into its making. The wealth of the enterprise, for there is none in the terminology of the financiers, is all contained between boards which enclose the texts.' From the beginning Miller drew about him not only the young writers but a variety of distinctive artists whose work lent distinction to the books. The list is impressive: Mia Cranwill, Elizabeth Rivers, Pauline Bewick, Leslie MacWeeney, Ruth Brandt, Norah McGuinness, Anne Yeats, Juanita Casey, Jack Coughlin, Tate Adams, Louis le Brocquy, S.W. Hayter, Eric Patton, Leonard Baskin, Bernard Childs and others.

The price paid for Miller's high ideals was commercial failure. The beautiful book, what Louis le Brocquy calls 'the thing itself', did not make money. What money the Press made came mainly from various printing commissions. Miller instinctively put quality first; it was the ideal that drove him through many lean years. The reward came in the appearance of the book and in occasional heart-warming praise from reviewers. Miller was not a good businessman. Even the overseas distribution and co-publication arangements that ensured a wider audience for his writers were not made on terms advantageous to Dolmen. Regrettably, as Rory Brennan notes, the Press never received adequate funding, and as a consequence 'the writer was often treated as the weakest link in the printer-to-bookseller chain'. The Press did not and could not support a writer, could not provide an advance, and seldom paid royalties, however modest. John Montague says he never received royalties and Thomas Kinsella comments on the lack of transparency in the Press's finances. Miller did not seem to appreciate how humiliating this was, and it has not been a good legacy for publishers.

Trained as an architect, he was a multi-talented man, something of a Renaissance figure in his range of interests and in his advocacy of the arts. He was founder-director and set-designer of the Lantern Theatre, designed sets for the Abbey in productions of Sean O'Casey and W.B. Yeats, became President of the Irish branch of PEN, created the design for *The Roman Missal*, was a member of the philately advisory committee for An Post, and the founding President of Clé, the Irish Book Publishers' Association. His interest in the theatre and in Yeats was constant. A large proportion of the Dolmen list is devoted to Yeats, including the *Yeats Centenary Papers*, which he had commissioned as a series of articles, and his own work on Yeats and the theatre: *The Noble Drama of W.B. Yeats*.

That he was admired and respected is evident from essays in this collection. Kathleen Raine, whose poetry and work on Yeats he published, regretted being unable to contribute to this book and wrote: 'Liam was a great artist of book production and I am honoured to have been among his authors of the Dolmen Press. Liam's work was a last expression of the Irish Renaissance which W.B. Yeats would have known how to appreciate. He was a lovely man, and very discerning in his choice of books and authors, and I remember him with deep affection.' He was, she wrote in another letter, 'a *great* publisher, and a man of deep culture, besides his charm, whose work would have delighted W.B.Y.'.

This collection begins and ends with an obituary — with John Calder's tribute to a fellow-publisher and Thomas Kinsella's graveside oration to a man who had made a difference to him and to his generation. Kinsella's final words — 'And he has left us great example' — conclude this commemoration.

M.H.

LIAM MILLER: OBITUARY

JOHN CALDER

Liam Miller, founder and publisher of the Dolmen Press, died on 17 May aged sixty-three after a long illness. He was everyone's favourite Irish publisher, an enthusiast for fine literature and fine books who seemed to belong to an earlier and gentler age, a gentleman of the old school. Ireland has produced many great writers, but most of them have left their native country behind and found publishers abroad. Liam created a link, kept in touch with such wild geese as Samuel Beckett so that some of his work (French translations) could appear on the Dolmen list, commissioned translations of Gaelic classics from leading poets, brought back into print distinguished Irish authors who had been neglected, and made contemporary Irish culture part of the European.

Originally a printer, he was a book designer of rare taste, oblivious to commercial considerations, who was often asked to design books outside

Ireland. He was at one point designer to the Vatican, for whom he printed missals and other liturgical publications. At times his printing-works subsidized his publishing, but the long postal strike of the seventies created great hardships for a publisher who depended on the mails for the bulk of his sales. The list diminished in recent years in number of titles produced but never in quality.

He was founding president in 1970 of Clé, the Irish publishing association, at what proved to be the start of a period of rapid expansion for Irish publishing. It was Liam Miller who persuaded Irish publishers to co-operate in the international Frankfurt Book Fair, obtained Irish government money to pay for it, and Irish whiskey from Jameson's to entertain visitors there.

Among his publishing achievements will be remembered Thomas Kinsella's translation of *The Táin*, the great Irish epic, many beautiful volumes of poetry, many collections of new Irish writing and modern editions of the Holinshed histories. As a writer he brought new scholarship to Irish criticism and his book on Yeats did much to revive interest in the plays. The post office asked him to design the stamps for the Yeats centenary.

But it was as a man that he will be most missed. He was never happier than among writers, artists and other publishers. He had an enormous acquaintanceship, and even those who met him only once felt they made a friend for life. Prodigal with time and hospitality, he made the international publishing community aware of Irish books and Irish literature, and his editions will long be a bibliophile's delight. He travelled everywhere, often just to be present at an Irish occasion in Toronto, Berlin or San Francisco, so it is not surprising that the Dolmen Press, a small quality publisher, should be as well known internationally as many long-established names.

First published in *The Bookseller*, 22 May 1987.

THE THING ITSELF

LOUIS LE BROCQUY

For many years I followed the devoted publishing activities of Liam Miller, which gave form to an endless series of literary works in Ireland that might otherwise have been ignored in their time; publications that included a number of significant discoveries made by my mother, Sybil le Brocquy, regarding Swift, Stella and Vanessa.

My own experience of *The Táin* remains one of the greatest adventures of my artistic life, revealed as it was by Thomas Kinsella's inspired translation and by Liam's determination to give a new coherent meaning to that unique proto-historic fantasy. Already translated into German and French, Kinsella's *Táin* has most recently been introduced in Spanish within Mexico to the excited acclaim of the poet Alberto Blanco and his colleagues.

Liam Miller belonged to that small band of wholly disinterested enthusiasts who enrich our lives. He was an artist enraptured by a vision of perfection for its own sake, by an overriding concern for *the thing itself.* I believe the final work Liam produced was a limited edition of Joyce's *Dubliners,* for which I made drawings. I shall not forget his last days in the wonderfully humane care of Our Lady's Hospice, free of pain and clear in his thought, still eagerly planning the perfect form of a publication he was unsure he would live to see.

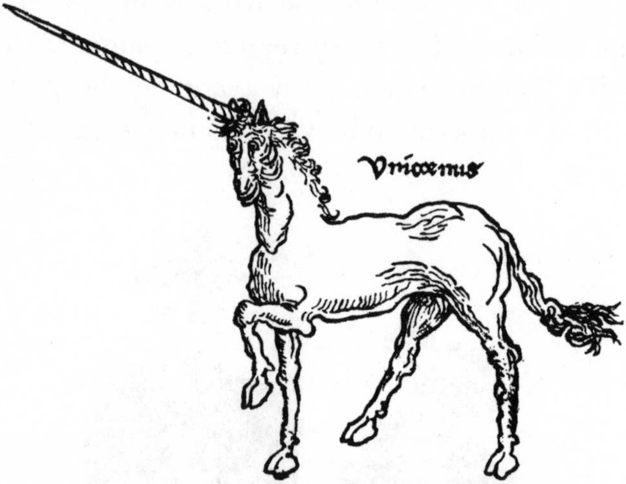

THE BRAZEN HORN

A NON-BOOK FOR THOSE WHO,
IN REVOLT TODAY,
COULD BE IN COMMAND TOMORROW

BY DENIS JOHNSTON

TWO INTERVIEWS WITH LIAM MILLER

I

Liam Miller with Kevin Casey,
RTÉ Radio One, 21 September 1976

KC: Perhaps the most distinguished of all Irish publishing houses is the Dolmen Press, which this year celebrates twenty-five years of existence. Since its foundation in 1951 the Dolmen Press has won an outstanding reputation not only for publishing the work of some leading Irish poets but for issuing them in a format and to a standard that has made most of their books collectors' items. Throughout its twenty-five years the moving force behind Dolmen has been Liam Miller. I asked him about the start of this company. Had it been a hand press?

LM: It was a hand press. I came to set up the Dolmen because I grew up in a generation — I was at college during the war here — I grew up with young writers who had no hope of ever being published. I worked in architecture in London for some years and bought a lot of books, read a lot of books and looked at the London scene and decided that, you know, for a lot of these Irish people there was at that time no hope in London. So I came back to Ireland, worked in architecture and founded a hand press, which literally was stored under the bed for a while, and printed a book. Had we not succeeded with our first book, my wife and I would have perhaps given up and gone into something else at that time.

KC: What was that first book?

LM: The first book was a book of ballads by Sigerson Clifford, whose work as a dramatist I had known — I had worked with him on his early plays, I had presented one of them at the old Peacock theatre, I had designed one of them in Belfast when it was produced during the war years. He had produced these ballads about the travelling people and I felt they were very good. In fact they are still very popular, one hears them recited every now and then on radio programmes. At that time people hadn't heard much about the travelling people as an ethnic thing. Clifford's stuff seemed to me to be very sympathetic, and to place them in a context in Ireland made his book very worthy. And this was a successful little book, it sold out its five hundred modest copies in a few weeks and we got on to other things. Later on Macmillan took over the ballads from us and the book made quite an impact as something coming from Ireland five or six years after we had done the first group from Dolmen.

KC: So, that was the start. Had your interest in typography and bookmaking as such preceded your involvement in publishing?

LM: My interest in typography was not really an interest in typography, I think it was an interest in order. My architectural training — how to sharpen a pencil and that kind of thing — had given me some sort of design discipline, and my approach to printing a book was to do something simple and honest and four-square and straight which our first book, may I say, wasn't at all. It suffered from all the pimples and all the other eruptions that that kind of apprentice effort always does.

KC: Were you very conscious of the tradition, say, of the Cuala Press?

LM: Not really. I knew of the Cuala Press. It wasn't until a few years later that I really made a study of the Cuala Press.

KC: Does hand printing mean literally that — that you set it up by hand?

LM: Yes, it can mean that you set up the type by hand, you assemble the pages by hand, and pray to God you don't drop the thing because you have maybe four and a half thousand separate little bits of metal. You actually succeed in getting them on the bed of the press and then you take your impressions. I chose Caslon as a typeface because I thought it was simple and classical, and it was available through type founders in Dublin at that time. We used this for our first books.

KC: Even the production of a very short book would take a long time.

LM: It can take a long time. In fact, my early effort after sweating out two or three books at Dolmen, setting them by myself or with my wife's help, was to invite the poets whom we had chosen and whose works we wanted to publish to come and help out in the evenings.

I've always had a concern for graphic design.

I think typography may have come later. You know, I liked the people who were trying to express themselves through graphics at that time, people like Michael Morrow, Michael Biggs and so on in Dublin. And I met them in cafés and asked them would they try to do something, cut a linocut, or do a line drawing. And a lot of our early books were illustrated by these people. I'm very proud to have worked with them. Later, as we became more professional or more slick or more whatever you like to call it, the opportunity of using graphic design diminished. You know, we had different problems facing us and different challenges in our publishing and printing life.

KC: And were you able to employ people who shared your own interest in the craft of printing?

LM: We weren't able to employ anyone for years and years. We did it all ourselves, with a lot of help given in odd moments at weekends. I continued to work for my bread and butter for perhaps about six years after we founded the press, and therefore it might be regarded as an amateur activity though it occupied perhaps more of the hours of my week than my bread-and-butter job.

KC: One notices throughout the years that your list has shown a fairly heavy commitment to certain writers. To Austin Clarke perhaps in particular, to both putting him into print and bringing him back into print, and to studies of Yeats.

LM: Well, I think one earns loyalty. Let's say the pattern follows a process whereby one takes on somebody — I would like to mention Kinsella here because he was the first new Irish talent I took on. We published his very first pamphlets. In fact we were publishing Kinsella for three to four years before he produced a collection of poems or a slim volume, if you like to call it. If an author has the right kind of rapport with the publisher, this loyalty is a lifelong endeavour. As others come along, Montague, and so on. And Austin, whom we persuaded to gather all the pamphlets he had issued at the Bridge Press, produced *Later Poems*, and from then on we were Austin's publisher.

KC: That's a kind of relationship that, I suppose, can hardly exist in more commercial publishing. A kind of sympathy between a publisher and …

LM: I think it does exist. You know, I think of Sam Beckett, whom I know quite well, and his publishers, both in London and in New York. He has two publishers in London, two main publishers in London, and one in New York. All of these have a personal friendship with him.

KC: You were bringing out Austin Clarke, it occurs to me, at a time when it could hardly have been profitable to do so; it obviously represented a commitment on the part of Dolmen to a major Irish writer whose reputation hadn't been fully recognized by that time.

LM: Well, I think Austin's reputation was dormant. I think my stand in relation to this was something which I learned over my first, let's say, apprentice years in publishing, about the peculiar position of Ireland in the publishing world. The Ireland I chose to publish in is Anglo-Ireland. You know, I think publishing in Irish is a totally separate thing, it's subsidized and insular, it's bounded, surrounded by water, confined to our island. But to see what impact writing in English from Ireland could make, I realized quite early on that one had to form friendships or liaisons in the bigger English-speaking world, because in my experience — and, I think, at a rough guess from my colleagues — the publisher of creative literature in English from an Irish base must export sixty to seventy per cent of his sales.

KC: And the finely produced book, such as we have come to expect from Dolmen, can it hope to play its part in an increasingly difficult climate for publishing?

LM: I don't deliberately produce finely produced books. To me every book is an individual problem. Certain titles have a built-in limitation. The audience for a certain title will be limited to a certain number of people. Sometimes, this will be something which proves the spearhead of a widening influence, as with Kinsella's *Táin*. At the time we did *The Táin* we estimated the market, we consulted with our distributors in England and America, and came up with the magic figure of one thousand seven hundred and fifty copies as being the expected market. Kinsella produced a work of such imaginative, creative and academic skill that this first edition exhausted itself in a few weeks. And the book got its second lease of life in the Oxford paperbacks which have sold many many thousands of copies since then. And this particular book, which justifies in my mind the entire Dolmen enterprise, has just begun to go into other languages.

II

Liam Miller with Andy O'Mahony, RTÉ Radio One, 23 August 1981

AO'M: In tonight's programme, the Dolmen Press, the particular success of which entitles it to a prominent place not merely in Irish publishing but in the cultural history of the country in the last quarter of a century. Its founder and driving force is Liam Miller.

LM: I grew up in a generation of Irish people where the young writer had to look to London for publication. Going through college with these people made me conscious of the fact that some of of them just didn't have a chance in London. I wanted to do something about bringing them out in their own country because I believed that the publication of a writer from Ireland in Ireland was an important thing, to give him a sense of identity with his own country, but also for the national pride of the country in an international sense, that our writers should at least be ushered into the world from Ireland.

AO'M: Well, what was your own background, you had trained as an architect …

LM: Trained as an architect, worked for awhile in Dublin, worked with Michael Scott, Luan Cuffe, with Noel Moffett, then went to London. I worked for about three to four years in London. Mainly at the end of the war period we were working on restorations of, you know, damaged properties and that, there wasn't much new building going on. But I did some theatre club work and read a lot, and I'd say those years in London formed a lot of my ideas. I think exposure to a culture outside your own country is very good for you when you're a young fellow. So when we came back to live in Ireland in 1950, I suppose the germ of the idea of publishing Irish writers was there, and by the following summer we had, my wife and I, formed some plans to bring out a book. And we brought out a book, and if it hadn't succeeded, I'm quite convinced, we would have stopped there and looked for some other outlet for our energies, but as we managed to recover whatever we put into that one, something else followed on.

AO'M: There must have been incredible excitement at the beginning. What are your memories?

LM: Incredible doubts and hesitations because we had only a rudimentary idea as to how printing happened. I'm sure that a little more knowledge would have put us off, you know. We went and bought font and type and set up a page and printed off that and cut up a whole ream of large paper with a sort of kitchen carving knife into the kind of sheets our little hand press would take, and printed the pages two at a time. Some of them were very badly inked, and an incredible amount of labour went into it, but it was all, I suppose, an excitement to us at the time. We learned as we went along and, I think, we managed to improve from our early start.

AO'M: It'd be very much a part-time activity …

LM: Oh, very much, I mean, all this was done in the evenings, and at weekends, and then, when we came to know some of the young poets around Dublin and were looking at their writings, we'd invite them in of an evening and they might have to fold sheets or stitch pamphlets or even set a bit of type. In fact, Tom Kinsella set some of his first poems, his second book, with his own hand, to print in the early pamphlet editions of his things that we did.

AO'M: That was *Three Legendary Sonnets*?

LM: Yes, yes, his sonnet book.

AO'M: And of course, you have had a long association with Tom Kinsella since then.

LM: Yes, we published his first book and we have published everything of his ever since and worked with him for many years on the big project which was *The Táin*.

AO'M: Without Louis le Brocquy ...

LM: Louis came in later. I mean, *The Táin* was planned, I think, as an idea in our second year at the Press, about 1952. Just after we had done Tom's first pamphlet of poems we then did his translation of the Deirdre story, *The Sons of Usnech*. And from that came the idea that some day we would do a whole *Táin*, put the epic into print for this century; that took, I think, about fifteen years before it came out, from '54 to '69, something like that. And over the years Tom worked slowly with this because he was earning his living at that time in the civil service in Dublin. And, then, when he went to America it wasn't until sometime in the 1960s that he was able to get a period of a few months to go and crystallize the whole book. And then spent years polishing it.

Louis, who had illustrated an early broadside for us in 1953, I asked him sometime in the middle sixties would he like to work on *The Táin*. And why our first edition came off magnificently was that Louis was — for most of the year before the book came out — in Dublin, Tom had a sabbatical from his American university, and we were all able to work together and put the book together in a kind of ideal situation that very rarely happens and I don't think it's ever happened to me before or since. We could set up type, plan the illustrations into the pages of type, work with the author's corrections, the positioning of the poems on the page, and then finally, you know, take a few days off for the three of us when the work was at press while the book was being bound, and go and visit all the scenes from the itinerary in the ancient manuscript.

AO'M: You did *The Táin* in a number of editions.

LM: There was a hardback in late 1969. And then the Oxford University Press took on the paperback, and they've been printing it ever since; we do the paperback in Ireland and they do the paperback in the rest of the world. And at the moment I am planning a return to the original drawings. In the 1969 hardback there is something like a hundred and thirty-nine Louis le Brocquy drawings. And in the paperback version which has been widely sold ever since there is only something like a quarter of that number.

AO'M: Yes, you hear of a portfolio of lithographs of that time …

LM: Yes, and I am now planning to do a library edition, not limited but, you know, a hardback of a larger page size which will accommodate the marginal illustrations, all of which were left out and which were very relevant.

AO'M: When you talk about paperback, in a way it runs counter, it seems to me, to the very idea of what you're about because I would imagine that your press, the Dolmen Press, is very much geared to people who are going to buy the hardback and have it as a kind of rare, special edition.

LM: Well, the hardback as we know it is really a kind of an English phenomenon. The case-bound, cloth-covered book is really an English invention. The French tradition is still to do a paper-covered book.

AO'M: You say a soft cover …

LM: A kind of soft cover. You see, we have to start thinking twice about paperbacks today. I mean on the one hand there's the mass-market paperback such as those produced for the Poolbeg series and Mercier. These are the two main Irish series, which are mass-produced paperbacks with the pages all glued together, so-called perfect bound. And then you have the thread-sewn, paper-covered book, and the French tradition is, if you like the book enough you go and have your binder cover it in something more durable. The readymade cover, hardcover, as I said, was a British invention which has become the sort of traditional norm in Ireland, England and America. But not necessarily elsewhere in the world.

AO'M: No, I mean, I'm not knocking the paperback, but given the emphasis of your press and publishing, it seems in a sense at odds with it. That's all I'm saying.

LM: No, I don't think so. I mean, our object has been, within our own terms of reference, of course, to make the books as widely available as we can, and a lot of our poetry, in fact, came out in paper covers originally. This now has become almost internationally the norm in poetry. The slim volume and cloth boards of the 1930s has vanished.

AO'M: So what percentage of your work, overall, since '51 has appeared in paperback, would you say?

LM: Perhaps a third of the books have come out in paper covers over the years.

AO'M: See, there is a sense, isn't there, which I notice in bookstores, that if there's a choice between a hardback and a paperback — for example, take the *Duanaire* which you did recently. The bookseller I went to said to me, 'Uh, uh, no, I won't let you, I won't let you take the paperback, I've got a hardcover inside here', the implication being this is the Dolmen Press, it's rare quality and so on. Do you know the kind of point I'm making?

LM: Oh, yes, but in that particular case, I feel there is the need for the longer shelf life of a hardbound. The *Duanaire,* which we do in what we call a split edition, some copies covered in paper covers and some in hardback, I think fills a need. Libraries buying a paperback, where they have to give it a shelf life and durability, would have to pay far far more to take it to a binder than we do by mass producing a hardback for them. It is a service really to the library trade to produce that kind of a case-bound hardback nowadays because, I think, most of the average book buyers are quite happy to buy the paper-covered copy. Particularly true the way prices are escalating.

AO'M: Yes, indeed — the 1969 edition of *The Táin* was in the ten-pound region, wasn't it?

LM: It was, yes.

AO'M: Nine fifty-nine. I bought *Holinshed's Chronicle* recently for, I think, about fifty pounds, a similar kind of book, you have a copy of it there.

LM: But the actual cost of manufacture has escalated about five times in that decade, you know.

AO'M: Have you ever been pleasantly surprised at the kind of response you've had to a particular limited edition?

LM: Yes, one in particular. Quite recently we did Professor O'Meara's translation of the voyage of Saint Brendan from the medieval Latin, which we did as a limited edition. It was one of the few books we did in full leather and with coloured illustrations; we did about fifty copies that way. And the little text got so well reviewed that we put it into a general trade edition about a year and a half later, and it has been selling happily ever since. And we are now considering taking that into a paperback edition also.

AO'M: When it comes to deciding what you are going to print, what are the main criteria as far as your house is concerned?

LM: Well, as far as my house is concerned, it boils down to my own personal tastes which sometimes might appear idiosyncratic. I believe in sort of a general Irishness for the Dolmen base; this means that we have done books on any kind of subject from an Irish writer and books on Irish subjects from writers all over the world. We have, for instance, the late Arland Ussher's books on Grimm's fairy tales and on the Tarot cards, and we have published a Japanese book on Yeats's drama, you know, so this covers both ends of the range. And we have poets who have developed in the whole Irish scene like Tom Kinsella, and Michael Hartnett, who now writes in Irish, and we've published people like John Kelleher of Harvard, who translates Irish poetry over there, and Vincent Buckley in Australia, whose themes are very Irish-influenced.

AO'M: And you've also published Kathleen Raine.

LM: And we've published Kathleen Raine. Well, Kathleen I came to know through our Yeats list originally, because she's one of the great scholars in Yeats and Blake studies. And she gave me a volume of poetry which I felt had spiritual affinities with Ireland. Kathleen is not an Irish poet, but the heritage of Yeats is clearly evident to me in her work, and I thought I would like to do this volume of verse, which we did in 1971 in association with Hamish Hamilton in London. That's another area I believe in, that we should have friendly associations with publishing houses abroad publishing from a small base like Ireland. Anyway, Kathleen's book, *The Lost Country*, was the first book of poems ever to receive the Smith Award, which is one of the most prestigious literary awards in England.

AO'M: Then it was rather an unusual book you did, I just see it there, Denis Johnston's *The Brazen Horn*.

LM: Well, I have always admired Denis's work and I had seen this, which he had drafted and printed in an earlier version privately, just a few copies for friends. It is, as he calls it himself, a non-book.

AO'M: It's a kind of long, speculative essay …

LM: It's a long, speculative essay on all sorts of things, time transference and the whole world today, and in some ways it is a sequel to his very successful book *Nine Rivers from Jordan*, which was ostensibly a war autobiography but appeared when you read into it to be much more.

AO'M: And, I think, it's a side of Johnston that many of us weren't aware of.

LM: I find this a very exciting book and I dip into it very often still. I think it has not been well enough recognized internationally yet, but some day, I feel, of all our books *The Brazen Horn* is one that is going to be discovered and become perhaps a cult book.

AO'M: You mentioned that again, the recognition abroad, and I want to return to a question I raised early about where your market is, and you just said it's abroad. Are we talking about America mainly?

LM: Well, yes, but I've had quite a good market in Britain ever since we started. For several years the Oxford University Press was my general distributor outside Ireland. And they also distributed our books in America for awhile, but since then I've used other outlets in America. This is also a belief I have in friendly co-operation with publishers, with the publishing industry.

AO'M: And I imagine you sell in the Far East, even if only to go by Parson's Bookshop ...

LM: Oh, yes, they sell in the Far East. And we sell quite a lot in Europe through German agents. The

Japanese tend to buy books about Irish landscape and about Yeats, subjects in which they have an interest. And in Germany quite a lot of sales, particularly in the field of our series on Irish theatre history. They're interested in recording the history of drama movements and of theatres, and, of course, *The Táin* was very successful in translation in both West Germany and East Germany.

AO'M: The theatre has been an abiding interest of your own.

LM: Well, I worked as a designer in the Abbey for a while and I worked with the little Lantern Theatre for many years in Dublin during its whole period of existence. And, of course, I compiled a book on Yeats's plays which took a long, long time, but I wanted to get my own ideas about Yeats's plays as drama rather than poetic set-pieces out.

AO'M: This is the thing you must be careful about, I suppose, the self-indulgence that you might allow yourself.

LM: One's own ideas and speculations must surface sometimes. The other thing I have committed myself was a little history of Dun Emer and the Cuala Press, which records the printing manifestation of the Yeats being, I suppose, because he inspired his sisters to found this very pioneering private press which is still running in Dublin.

AO'M: Is there any one big area that you think you've neglected?

LM: Well, one area which I was very conscious of being rather an empty one during all the earliest years of the Press was the area of creative fiction writing. We did, of course, do several works of fiction — Austin Clarke's novel *The Bright Temptation* and Juanita Casey's two novels, both of which were successful, and a collection of folktales, *Tales of the West of Ireland* by James Berry, which still continues to reprint almost annually. The emergence of a couple of publishing houses which are concentrating on modern Irish fiction writing, I think, makes the balance much healthier for Ireland. One thing I found in Irish publishing is that one does not get the rivalries and tensions one senses in publishing in Britain and America particularly …

AO'M: Why is that?

LM: Well, the publishing community is small enough to be a kind of a brotherhood. And, you know, there isn't the kind of mad scramble after one or the other property here.

AO'M: I suppose one of the advantages of that kind of smallness is that you can co-operate to free certain kinds of costs.

LM: Oh, absolutely we co-operate; for instance, I co-operate with several other publishers in Irish Bookhandling Ltd, which does our warehousing and billing and which is a kind of exercise that might for a small publisher take an unduly big portion of the overhead costs, but if shared it does not take the same proportion of the costs.

AO'M: There are advantages in the smallness.

LM: There are great advantages in the smallness. At the same time, I think there must be more dialogue about things like VAT and various public issues which affect us all. And keep the publishing scene happy and healthy.

The transcripts of both interviews have been edited lightly for the sake of clarity and readability.

'BELOVED DOLMEN'

LIAM BROWNE

I first became aware of the Dolmen Press in 1955 when Liam and Jo, his wife and my sister, lived on Sion Hill Road, Drumcondra. They had two children then, Liam Óg and Máire Óg, whom the local children thought of as being members of the Óg family. I would visit with them and see Liam and Jo with ink-stained hands and having their friends folding sheets of printed paper or packing books. At that time they had a small Adana platen press, which could take a paper size of ten by eight inches. They had previously been printing on a small wooden press donated by a friend.

Liam wanted to develop the Press and asked me if I would be interested in working with them. As the firm I was working with then was closing down, my father suggested that I should become involved and he supplied the funds for me to have a one-third interest.

At this time Liam and Jo went to live in

Silchester Park in Glenageary, and it was there that I commenced my involvement with Dolmen. My first assignment was to hand-set the type for the broadsheet 'The Mines of Siberiay' by Arland Ussher (1956). Liam instructed me in the use of the hand press, and like Liam and Jo I had to be able to do whatever was necessary.

As the volume of work increased, it was no longer viable to operate from the house and we made our move to the basement of 23 Upper Mount Street. There we were able to have an Albion hand press, as illustrated by Ruth Brandt in *Dolmen XXV*, which at that time must have been eighty years old. We also had a foot-treadle Arab platen machine which could take a sheet size of fifteen by ten inches. We later had a motor attached, which eliminated the hard labour. We also had a manual guillotine. Not the most up-to-date machinery available, but all that we could afford.

At this time, in 1958, we were undertaking commercial work such as small posters and programmes for theatres, stationery and catalogues. I remember well printing the programmes for Tennessee Williams' *The Rose Tattoo* with Liam and bringing them over to the Pike Theatre, which was only a stone's throw from us. Liam also obtained the contract to print the programmes for the Royal Ballet's appearance at the Theatre Royal. It was way beyond our capacity to produce the numbers required, but with the help of family and friends who were called upon to assist in folding and stapling we just about managed. I recall going to the ballet with Liam one evening and going back to work through the night to hand-set the programme, the cast list for the following evening only having been given to us after that evening's performance.

As we became known as printers specializing in small print runs, with Liam's reputation as a designer and typographer, our client list increased. We employed four people to assist us whom we trained ourselves. We purchased a new Heidelberg cylinder press that could take a sheet size of thirty by twenty inches. This allowed us to undertake printing for the National Gallery, the David Hendriks Gallery, the Dawson Gallery, Cadenus Press and similar clients for whom we printed for many years. We later became a trade union house.

The number of Dolmen publications was increasing annually, which necessitated the leasing of premises at Herbert Place that were used as the publishing office with Mount Street solely for printing. A major difficulty was trying to juggle the machine times with such limited printing capacity. Liam gave authors licence to alter their work time and again after it had been typeset. This was a major factor in cost overruns on many of our publications, but Liam, as publisher, was interested only in having the perfected work; cost was not the main consideration.

The most memorable editions for me were *Out of Bedlam* (1956), which I printed, hand-fed, on the Arab platen, with its wonderful Elizabeth Rivers wood engravings; *Riders to the Sea* (1968) with the Tate Adams engravings printed in colour; and *The Táin* (1969), which I oversaw, for the active participation of Thomas Kinsella and Louis le Brocquy and their attention to detail during the printing process.

In the early seventies Dolmen was under financial pressure and a decision was made to reorganize. New shares were issued, to which I subscribed along with some 'Friends of Dolmen', and Thomas Kinsella and Alec Reid were appointed directors. It was decided to reduce the publishing overheads, Herbert Place was vacated, the printing and warehousing would operate from North Richmond Street, and Liam would work mainly from his home in Mountrath, Co. Laois.

Our printing process was letterpress, but through the years lithographic printing, or litho, had made great technical progress, with typesetting on film which could be produced more economically than hot metal, and with the scope to print on papers that letterpress could not handle. We were faced with a situation where we would have to re-equip and re-train staff. As we did not have the funds to do so we decided, reluctantly, to close our printing operation. Liam would continue to produce Dolmen publications and use various printing houses. I more or less ceased to have any involvement although I was still a shareholder.

The difficulty Dolmen always had was that it was underfunded. Liam's vision of Dolmen could not be realized without the means, and while there were some patrons, and the Arts Council funded various projects annually, this was never sufficient to do other than keep the company afloat. Liam was a very talented person, with diverse interests. I often wonder what his achievements would have been had he been involved with a larger enterprise with the funds to see all his ideas to fruition — but then he would not have had, as he would say after a glass or two of wine, his 'beloved Dolmen'.

Liam and Jo were wonderful hosts and their homes at Glenageary, Baggot Street, Fitzwilliam Square and then Mountrath were seldom without visitors, either staying or having a meal. Jo is an excellent cook and Liam would have ideas for the meal, helping with the shopping and generally doing whatever was required to make their guests' visit enjoyable, as my own family appreciated when we spent a couple of memorable Christmases at Mountrath.

He had a way with people, being able to converse with them on whatever level made them comfortable. His interests, which included philately, numismatics, ballet, painting, architecture and design, gave him a wealth of knowledge to draw on in discussing any of the above, but on going into a public house he could also discuss the quality of the pint with the locals.

Liam's health began to deteriorate in 1984, but it was not until 1986 that he was diagnosed with cancer. He stayed at home, where he was tended to by Jo and comforted by his children Liam, Máire, Kate and Jane for as long as was possible. He then went to Our Lady's Hospice, Harold's Cross, where he died on 17 May 1987.

At his funeral mass there were many tributes from people who had known and worked with Liam on different projects, and all expressed their admiration for this gifted man. The final tribute from the priest officiating at the mass was to Liam's interest and knowledge of Church liturgy and to the fact that the altar missal being used had been designed by Liam Miller.

TIME WAS AWAY

TERENCE BROWN

I do not recall whether it was Alec Reid or myself who first suggested that we jointly edit a book on the poet Louis MacNeice. It had been Trevor West (TCD mathematician, senator, sportsman) who had introduced us in the Lincoln Inn. Although Alec's first literary love was Samuel Beckett, he immediately took an interest in the fact that I had written a thesis on MacNeice and was preparing a critical study for the press. He was a MacNeice man as well as a sensitive and compelling interpreter of Beckett's drama. With a few pints taken he could be prevailed upon to speak from memory MacNeice's marvellous love lyric from 'Trilogy for X', 'And love hung still as crystal', or parts of 'Leaving Barra' (written for the painter Nancy Sharp). Alec had been to Oxford during the war years and had a strong fellow feeling for the Anglo-Irish poet who had preceded him there just over a decade earlier.

Alec's book on Beckett (*All I can manage, more than I could*) had been published by the Dolmen Press in 1968 and he was pretty sure that Liam Miller would be willing to consider myself and himself as joint editors of a memorial book for Louis (with Alec it was always Sam and Louis), who had not, he felt, ever had his due in Dublin. I was not so sure. I associated the Press with the work of Austin Clarke and Thomas Kinsella (and I still remember the Dolmen publication of *Nightwalker* as a moment of great personal excitement as modern Dublin was fully entered in the Irish poetic mindscape). Was it likely he would take very seriously a young unproven Man from the North with an unfashionable enthusiasm (this was about 1970; MacNeice's English reputation was then in the doldrums, his Irish reception, such as it was, largely a Northern matter)?

I could not have been more wrong. Liam took to the project immediately and from our earliest planning meetings simply assumed that I was up to the job (perhaps Alec had put in a good word, based on what I cannot imagine). Our three-way discussions soon became intriguing sessions in which Alec and I would discuss aspects of Louis's achievement which should be covered and possible contributors, with Liam as a kind of inspirational presence. Long before e-mail or even a credible telephone service, he took for granted that anyone could be contacted, however far-flung they might be. Meetings, which rarely began at the appointed hour, lasted for ages as one or other long-distance call was put through from public house or hotel bar. They almost invariably took place in such places where Liam was in conference with some author, artist, or visitor on a pilgrimage to Dublin. Our book, about which I had become anxiously possessive, was only a small part of what was obviously a variegated range of activities all centred on Liam, who had a creative calm equal to any author's or editor's anxiety. His attitude was clear: a book could not be rushed; it would appear in its own good time and it would be worth waiting for.

So wait I did. Over several years the manuscript slowly accreted. It was a coup when Auden allowed his memorial address for MacNeice to be reprinted. Liam was keen that we should have a piece from Stephen Spender, and one Christmas Eve I found myself phoning (from a public phone box no less; a young lecturer then could scarcely afford the rent on a phone) a number Liam or Alec had given me where the former communist poet of the 'pylon school' was spending the holiday season. I was put through to the Château Rothschild. Summoned from the *premier cru,* the great man confirmed that he would not be contributing. A saturnine smile flickered across

Liam's sallow features when I reported on this unsatisfactory exchange.

Liam was not principally a verbal man, though his business was so involved with words. One sensed in his company the artist's tactile intimacy with the material world, the designer's eye for form, dimension, spatial relationship. Yet his own involvement with theatre design made him exactly the man to write a very valuable book on Yeats's dramaturgy. His *The Noble Drama of W.B. Yeats* (1977) remains a monument to his dedication to another master craftsman. It is written with exact passion, combining scholarship with advocacy in an act of generous respect.

It was precisely such generosity and respect that he extended to MacNeice in the short celebration that he contributed to *Time Was Away: The World of Louis MacNeice,* which he published in 1974. A year before, he had presented a reading of Louis's poems in the Peacock. About this time I remember the diffidence with which he offered a piece to us and was surprised at his nervousness, when it came along, that it might not suit. In the event he saluted with characteristic modesty a man whose conversation he had grown to love and whose last play, *One for the Grave,* he had helped as designer to the Abbey stage. In his piece for *Time Was Away* he associated MacNeice with Leonardo's Renaissance man and wrote of his feelings for a 'great Irish creative being'. I feel similarly about Liam Miller, and I was privileged in my youth to have had the opportunity to see him at work and to have my first book appear from his remarkable Press.

LIAM MILLER 1924–1987

An appreciation of his contribution to book design

JARLATH HAYES

In terms of his craft Liam Miller beat the computer by twenty years or so, just before Gutenberg's 'hot' metal became cold, before designing with type finished as a series of electronic pulses or before, typographically speaking, anaemia set in. Although he did not know it at the time, he came at an end of an era when in 1951 he hand-set his first Dolmen books. He was then twenty-seven.

They were bad times then in Ireland, particularly for architects and artists — some turned in desperation to arty sidelines and we had a plethora of good/bad/awful sculpture, pottery, wall hanging, ceramics. Why Liam turned to printing I have no idea, but certainly in his first infant editions there is little sign of any stopgap venture, no tiding over till things got better, no dilettante dabbling with a hand press. Warts and all, these first slim volumes show an extraordinary maturity and insight in a man who has just swapped his slide rule for a composing stick and who had few inspiring influences around him except perhaps the Three Candles and the Cuala Press.

Among the earliest efforts were poetry editions by Thomas Kinsella. Poetry is comparatively easy to set but deceptively difficult to position on the page, and a look at Richard Murphy's *The Archaeology of Love* (1955), though it is not well machined, shows how in such short experience his eye could triumph over the staid geometrical rules of copybook typography. Above all else his typographical attitude gave such distinction to his book design, although for a while understandably it tended to be somewhat formalized. But all in all, like William Morris he shook things up — Morris because of the awful things the technology of the time did to the printed page, Miller because he felt we could have done better — and this, I think, remained his abiding motivation, to redeem, improve and enhance. The result put him well apart and away above his contemporaries in book design and made Dolmen known from America to Australia.

His typography was pellucid; he loved and soaked himself in the post-incunabula period of

Garamond and Janson and from them, and by his own alchemy, he achieved a new grace and a civilized assurance which was fresh and original in the face of the degraded typography and wooden pages of the day.

His first city base was in Upper Mount Street, not far from Kinsella, with and for whom he produced the outstanding Peppercanister series. The move to Herbert Place marked the beginning of his 'heavier' titles, like the *Dolmen Text* series and Kinsella's translation of *The Táin*. Later there was the printing place at North Richmond Street complete with a Linotype specially adapted for book work, with matrices of his beloved Pilgrim, and on which compositor Jim Hughes set the monumental *Holinshed's Irish Chronicle 1577*. It was printed on an especially made paper and, though not machined to his satisfaction, was awarded a bronze medal at the International Book Design Exhibition at Leipzig in 1981.

Liam Browne, his brother-in-law and manager at North Richmond Street, saw all the work through the press, which relieved Miller of much of the day-to-day routine and gave him more time and less commuting to Mountrath. Indeed after the closure of the plant, which was also the warehouse of Irish Bookhandling, he returned to Mountrath and produced work of a much wider scale than before; he was now free to buy good print from the commercial houses and had access to a range of typesetters and ancillary services.

Mountrath was a period — all too short — of diversification: *Postage Stamps of Ireland 1922–1982,* which he compiled for the Department of Posts and Telegraphs; *The Dolmen Book of Irish Stamps; Harry Clark; Pictures of the Abbey* (Michael Ó hAodha); *Ireland Beyond the Pale;* the beginning of a series for children of which *The Comical Cat* is a superb example of its kind, set entirely in Hammer uncial which he introduced to Ireland in the early sixties; and, finally, his massive *Dubliners,* with illustrations by his old friend Louis le Brocquy and appropriately the subject of a tribute to Miller by RTÉ before he died.

His energy and single-mindedness were remarkable. He sought out the very best in materials, artwork and authors; he scoured France for genuine marbled endpapers and the North of Ireland for poplin to cover the Pope's Lectionary; found obscure paper-makers who could supply the correct grain; unearthed special founts for particular titling-caps and headings. His briefcase was a veritable mobile filing cabinet never containing less than a couple of titles in various stages of production, and many a Dolmen jacket design was doodled in a CIÉ rail car somewhere between Dublin and Mountrath.

To many, Dolmen seemed to exist for poetry

alone — true early on and for his own positively expressed reasons — but in time his stocklist included works on art, architecture, history, music, drama, theatre and topography as well as biography, criticism and even a little fiction — a fairly good indication of the subjects and scale of his interests.

By 1979 Dolmen had produced over two hundred and sixty titles, certainly not a bad output by any measurement, but round this period there was a detectable falling-off of quality, a run-of-the-mill look, somewhere an absence of his hand, possibly explained by the move to North Richmond Street and the need to support it with outside commercial work. His design never faltered but the finished work suffered a little because, I think, and Liam himself was aware, he was never fully equipped to machine and finish his books to a higher standard.

Apart from the Dolmen connection he was a recognized Yeatsian authority, and after Clarke, Montague and Kinsella it is Yeats who features high in his annual book lists, primarily through the *New Yeats Papers*, a series which deals with many aspects of the poet's life, work and background and which up to 1978 had reached XVII with Kathleen Raine's *From Blake to 'A Vision'*. Earlier in 1967 he began his history of the Cuala Press; he completed it in 1973 and, at the request of Michael

Yeats, helped in the revival of the Press itself.

Of all his pursuits, and there were many — typesetter, printer, publisher, editor, writer, set-designer, Yeatsian scholar, philatelist — typography remained his one tool to serve them all. Ever conscious of the wispy subtleness of the craft, he achieved something of the art of hiding the art, that shadowy point where even the uninitiated feels something beyond the commonplace. He also achieved, by design or not, a restoration to Dublin of some of her past fame as a book-producing centre, and he gave impetus and advice to an up-and-coming crop of young publishers. He designed, too, for other publishers — the most notable work and, I think, the finest being *The Roman Missal,* commissioned by the Irish Hierarchy.

Liam knew his worth and he had no reason not to; his success was well deserved; his reputation will remain as will our debt to him. He showed us that a book is a lot more than a wad of paper between two boards.

First published in *Books Ireland,* Summer 1987.

LIAM DOLMEN

JOHN MONTAGUE

I first heard of Liam Miller through an O'Meara cousin of mine from Longford, who was attending night classes at the National College of Art and staying in a digs in Dublin run by, I think, a Polish lady. He said that there was a very artistic young fellow from the midlands who was staying in the same digs and studying architecture, called Bill or William Miller.

When I met my future publisher at his basement offices in Upper Mount Street in 1956, he was definitely Liam, not Bill or William. An intense, dark-avised figure, he looked Jewish, or at least Eastern European, a pale unworldly scholar from another time and place, who had perhaps found refuge in Ireland. It was a time when scholars, like the palaeographer Ludwig Bieler, found a haven in places like the Institute of Advanced Studies, and Liam Miller seemed as exotic a savant as any of them.

In fact, he was a butcher's son from Mountrath in County Laois who had just founded a publishing house, and was dedicated to Irish poetry and drama in a way that had not been seen in Dublin since the early days of the Irish Literary Renaissance, the days of the Cuala Press and Maunsel and Roberts. In order to subsidize that ideal, he was also a job printer who took on most of the work that came his way. I did not observe him at the very beginning of his career, since I had embarked on my Grand Tour of America, but I had already heard positive reports of his dedication. It seemed he had discovered his vocation when he bought a small hand press, and fell in love with the lovely process of printing; years later he would describe, with a chuckle, how marvellously erotic the technical language of the trade was. And his growing sense of design probably came from his architectural training.

A literary or artistic movement is usually the conjunction of a constellation of several talents at the same time and place. And the foundation of the Dolmen Press coincided with the diffident first steps of Richard Murphy (*The Archaeology of Love*), Thomas Kinsella (*Poems*, and *Another September*) and myself (*Forms of Exile*). I remember a little congregation of us outside the basement press, and someone saying: 'Not a bad place to become the centre of Irish literature!' In fact it was an infant enterprise, and Liam was learning as he went along, so that the sour comments of Philip Larkin on his rejection were only partly justified. He refers in his letters to the Dolmen Press as a 'chicken-hearted institution', as indeed it was in the sense of age, slightly cocksure without yet being a fully grown Pathé rooster crowing its wares.

Since we lived around the corner from each other, it was natural that we should begin to work together. Indeed, we were so close by then I could judge Liam's mood by the hour he went down to the press, as well as his general gait of going, dark head up or down, briefcase borne lightly or like a load of lead. I understood his problems, trying to subsidize a small poetry press while supporting a young family, and while I was to have no children myself, I was sympathetic to his cares. But when he delayed publication of my first manuscript, I realized that his financial state was chronically constrained, and agreed to contribute to its appearance in 1958, with a donation of £40. It was nearly three weeks' salary in those days, but I was nearing the advanced age of thirty, with poems all over the place but no individual volume to my name.

I think that this may have helped to create an unease, an imbalance, in our financial relationship. And may also have led to my partly leaving Dolmen for MacGibbon & Kee, when Timothy O'Keeffe offered me my first real advance for

Poisoned Lands. In the long run, I don't regret this move, because it gave me an influence on their Irish list, as a first reader, from Anthony West's prose to Patrick Kavanagh's poetry. And another advance helped me to work on my short-story collection, *Death of a Chieftain*. While Timothy O'Keeffe had only a poor sense of the minutely complex world of poetry politics, he did his best by the stories, and for a young man intent on making a career as a writer, having an English publisher seemed a positive move.

But of course I never really left Liam, who had become a good friend, and whose creative generosity outweighed his financial uncertainties. We worked together on what was to become *The Dolmen Miscellany*, the first anthology of the then new Irish writing; I had an amused letter from Aidan Higgins about descending into the basement with the proofs and being impressed by the amount of beard he found there. And of course there was the private publication of my poem 'Like Dolmens Round My Childhood, the Old People' in 1960, after it had received a prize in Belfast. I have often wondered whether our obsession with standing stones was mutual, or was mine sparked off unconsciously by the name of his press. Or, more likely, the new interest in archaeology in Ireland, which I would satirize in the title story of *Death of a Chieftain*.

Our second personal collaboration was with my sequence of love poems, *All Legendary Obstacles* (1966), which came out at roughly the same time as Kinsella's *Wormwood*, as a Dolmen Edition. (Since I had recently edited the collected poems of Patrick Kavanagh, I was eager that Irish poetry should move from the peat to the private, which was also happening in our rapidly changing country as the cities burgeoned and factory farming replaced the old rural ways.) Though I was very close to the painter Barrie Cooke at the time, I am still startled by his sprawling cover design, which caused Tom Kinsella no end of mirth. He wanted to know how I thought poetry was being served by having a distinguished Irish professor copulating on the cover. Like a Rorschach blot, the inky incoherence of the design laid itself open to many interpretations.

When I came back from Paris to Dublin for editorial sessions, or Claddagh meetings, I would often stay with Jo and Liam in their house in 94 Lower Baggot Street. It was a splendid bohemian haven where all seemed welcome, singers like Ronnie Drew (I think he met his wife there), actors like Eamon Keane, John B.'s brother. Whatever the Millers had, they shared, with a joint (of meat) coming up from Mountrath at the weekend, and the kettle always on the boil. And occasionally they held parties, where I met a heroine of our childhood, Patricia Lynch, whose story *The Turf Cutter's Donkey* was in every Irish household, and who was accompanied by the socialist writer R.M. Fox. The editorial sessions were held in that front room immortalized by Cartier-Bresson, with Tom Kinsella and myself sharing eager plans, which a benevolent bearded Liam sought to orchestrate. It was a fascinating three-way dialogue among equals, and when Liam struck a financial rock in the mid-sixties we were able to organize a rescue committee which met in that same room.

So when I came to publish *A Chosen Light* (MacGibbon & Kee, 1967), I dedicated it to Liam, and to Garech Browne, whom I describe as 'friendly hosts', in the double sense of hospitality, and soldiers in the service of a new Irish aesthetic. And Liam and I had begun our most important collaboration, the publication of sections of *The Rough Field*. This was the kind of task he loved, finding a format for 'Patriotic Suite' (1966), which was partly a riposte to the overly nationalistic celebrations of that year. Hence the green cover with a Derricke illustration that Kinsella rightly saw as a parody of 'Reidy's Band', Seán Ó Riada's motley crew of traditional musicians in his Ceoltóirí Chualann. After the liturgical format of 'The Bread God', which embarrassed most Irish reviewers, came 'Hymn to the New Omagh Road' with its look of an old-fashioned accounting ledger. Perhaps too old-fashioned, so Liam replaced it with the open postcard format of 'A New Siege'. As these individual pamphlets appeared, I found myself going home to the North more and more, compelled by the burgeoning of the long poem, which paralleled a new political restiveness.

To work on a text with Liam was fascinating, a kind of intellectual dance. He experimented with various typefaces, lengths of page, and quality of paper, always inviting comment, seeking an ideal blend or marriage of the visual and the verbal. All those sections of *The Rough Field* are now collector's items, as is the first hardbound edition of the complete book. I cannot imagine anyone else responding so eagerly to the challenge of an unusual text, balancing the talents of both editor and publisher. I think that period may well be the apogee of Liam's achievement, when he was planning Kinsella's *Táin* and helping me plough *The Rough Field*.

Ironically, during what now seem to me the halcyon years of the Dolmen Press, both Kinsella and I were living mainly out of the country, Tom in Carbondale, Illinois or, later, Philadelphia, and myself in Paris or 'improbable California'. 'Life in Ireland without you and Tom', wrote Liam, 'is hell on a green isle.' But these lengthy absences seemed to make our partnership with him prosper, so that when we did meet, it was with the intensity and enthusiasm of real colleagues re-finding each other. In late 1970, or early 1971, Liam prompted me gently, 'Maybe you should begin to draw this long poem in. It can't go on forever, and every farmer needs a harvest.'

But I leap ahead. My friend Timothy O'Keeffe had lost his battle to preserve MacGibbon & Kee as an independent and creative publisher, and had been swallowed by Bernstein of Granada. So with *Tides* (1970), I had officially returned to Dolmen (Kinsella declared tartly that I should never have left). When Liam was on a visit to Paris to meet Beckett, I had introduced him to Bill Hayter, the engraver and printer, for whom I had done a sequence called 'Sea Changes'. They got along famously because both were demons for work, and Liam commissioned him to do a cover for *Tides*, with a female form swirling through water. My personal life was changing at the time, and I remember the excitement of working with Liam on the proofs in the old Majestic Hotel, where Berryman had begun his Dublin stay. Robin Skelton was there, the artist Jack Coughlin from Montague, Massachusetts, and the young woman who would become my second wife. We were all in high good humour, and that combination of hard work and hijinks was characteristic of almost all my dealings with Liam Dolmen.

Sometimes we met after work in Phil Ryan's pub

in Baggot Street, now absorbed into the inhuman, fashionably bleak façade of Ronnie Tallon's Bank of Ireland. It was a comfortable upper room, with a view across the street, a favourite watering hole for distinguished older writers like Kate O'Brien and Patrick Kavanagh, as well as some of the stray McDaid's young, hopefully plying Liam with manuscripts. For, after Kinsella, Murphy and myself, there was another generation, people like melancholy James McAuley, and the always exuberant James Liddy who was editing *Arena*, which fostered the post-*Collected* Kavanagh and printed an illustrated version of my *The Siege of Mullingar*. If the family were away, Liam liked nothing better than a brief descent into the whirlpool of McDaid's itself. There was Kavanagh in his corner, coughing and snorting, Myles hunched over his drink before heading abruptly home, the artist Seán O'Sullivan discoursing in French, and, of course, the Rathmines brigade, Pearse Hutchinson, the poet, and John Jordan, editor of *Poetry Ireland*. Leaning over John, trying to comprehend some intensely muttered intellectual message, I felt a warm flow of sour-smelling stout pour over my head. Turning in astonishment, I confronted a beaming Liam. 'You are John,' he explained with lunatic logic. 'And you are standing by Jordan.'

Liam also did his best to help our older writers,

introducing the later Austin Clarke to a larger audience and organizing celebrations for his seventieth birthday, including a small *Festschrift* with contributions by Ted Hughes, Christopher Ricks, Charles Tomlinson, Serge Fauchereau, as well as the usual Irish suspects. There was a launch party in a Baggot Street bar with the unfortunate name the Crooked Bawbee, where I made a clumsy speech in French and English, which brought the wrath of Padraic Colum down on my head. And Liam tried to be friendly with Kavanagh, who, after all, lived only up the way in Pembroke Road, but the other Old Master could be very irascible. Although once, when Liam was on his own, we brought back Kavanagh from the pub for a rest and a feed of bacon, sausage and eggs. I had just visited a doctor friend of mine who, when I was sleepless or despondent, would offer me samples from his medicine cupboard. One tablet made me feel particularly lively, and I asked the morose Kavanagh if he would like to try them. 'Only take one,' I cautioned. 'They're very strong.' Patrick returned to the pub, and swallowed the entire contents of the phial with compulsive fervour, washing it down with whatever drinks were going.

Next morning he was banging on Liam's door. 'Have you more of that stuff?' he pleaded. 'I loved it! I took off like a rocket!' Unfortunately, a dispute sprang up between himself and Liam, who was publishing a small edition of the text of Patrick's television *Self Portrait*, which had introduced the poet to a larger, more popular audience. Liam wanted to use some unbuttoned pictures of the poet sprawling or walking around his favourite haunt, Baggot Street Bridge, but Patrick was very sensitive about his dignity as a senior poet, especially now that some belated fame had come to him. He hated to be called 'Paddy' because of the stage-Irish implications, and he felt that a book cover showing him in cap and braces would perpetuate the unfortunate early impression of him as a 'rural bard'. So a new cover had to be found, but he remained suspicious of Liam's good intentions.

More than most publishers, Liam liked to be part of the action, and to meet his writers socially, which of course worked to the advantage of writers who lived in Dublin and could ease his solitary dedication with pleasant pub sessions. His brother-in-law, Liam Browne, dealt mainly with the commercial side of the business, leaving Miller largely free to focus on the editorial side. But I don't think he ever set up a proper mechanism for dealing with manuscripts, so it was into this trough that Seamus Heaney's early manuscript, 'An Advancement of Learning', fell. Very few people in Dublin, apart from myself, had yet heard of Heaney, Tom Kinsella was away in America, and my visits back were as irregular as inspiration. As for Liam, he could not attach a face to the name, and certainly never mentioned it to me, or, I believe, Tom. Not knowing of this early manuscript, I recommended Heaney to O'Keeffe at MacGibbon & Kee, but by that time Faber & Faber had already snapped him up. It is interesting to speculate how his career would have developed if Liam had had the good sense to ask my advice about this promising young voice from the North, but then Belfast, and the North generally, had not yet swung back into the Southern consciousness.

For Liam and most of his Dublin contemporaries, the North of Ireland barely existed except as a distant, thorny place. Even the published sections of *The Rough Field* could not persuade Liam that the North might foster other voices. I suppose that some of this had to do with Dublin's flickering new energy. From a moribund post-'Emergency' city, where dispirited poets drank in murky pubs, it was becoming artistically alive, with Liam as one of its leading lights. The last thing Southerners wanted in that new climate was to consider the unresolved 'Northern problem', which had been, by general unspoken consent, moved to the back burner. So the rejection of Seamus was a missed opportunity, with myself and Tom both out of the country, and Liam overwhelmed.

When I finally gathered in *The Rough Field*, at

Liam's behest (I had some vague plan of basing it on the thirteen months of the Old Year), we set out to find a visual equivalent. The opening section, 'Home Again', was also published separately, with a line drawing of the cauldron from County Tyrone in the National Museum, as a symbol of the prodigal's return. And we cast around for similar emblems for each section, but other images did not come so readily to hand. Nor did the idea of putting the already published sections together, with their varying typefaces and design, seem to work; instead of indicating the diversity of voices in the text, it looked like a typographical jumble. Then Liam triumphantly reproduced the Derricke engravings (one of which we had already used for 'Patriotic Suite'), which underlined the dialogue between present and past that is at the heart of the work. And the unusually large dimensions of the first edition was part of the effect, a blend of ledger and missal. My old English nemesis, the Poetry Book Society, did not think so: perhaps, as with the Australian poet Peter Porter, they detected what they considered a latent republicanism, failing to realize that the book is woven of many strands, including the psychic defeat of my patriot father. Besides, I did not fulfil their new expectations of an Irish poet, expectations that I, by helping to revive Kavanagh, had partly encouraged: while celebrating Patrick's country themes and imagery, I had hoped that succeeding Irish poets would move on, embracing personal, urban and indeed international subjects. It did not occur to me that Kavanagh's themes would harden into a formula, to which a new generation would be expected to hew. *The Rough Field* did not even get a Recommendation, and was tardily reviewed, although it would make its way into many editions.

A further dimension was added when Paddy Moloney arranged the traditional music implicit in the text for a public performance, first in the Peacock Theatre in Dublin, and then in London, at the Roundhouse in Chalk Farm, a performance recorded for Claddagh Records. Again, Liam helped to produce the dramatic version, and clearly enjoyed the task, working with a medley of actors like Pat Magee and Alun Owen, and writers like Benedict Kiely, Seamus Heaney and myself. For the theatre was another love of his, and his work in the Lantern, the basement theatre underneath the British Embassy in Merrion Square, was part of his fertile vision. Great publishers have a kind of diverse energy, and Liam was a sort of Dublin Diaghilev during the sixties and seventies, coaxing and arranging things into existence. I brought over a small shoal of French poets, like Michel Deguy, and it was under the light of the Lantern that John Berryman gave the only public reading of his Dublin *hegira*. Together, we concocted a plan for an All-Ireland Poetry Festival, or *Fleadh na bFilí*, with backings from my old employers, the Irish Tourist Board, but it fell apart when I could not get the Russian Embassy in London to send us some Muscovite bards to complete the picture.

When we met in Dublin in the sixties, I was either coming from Paris or going to California, and our meetings had an almost hectic quality, the pleasure of friends and colleagues coming together briefly and intensely. After I returned to Ireland in the seventies we met more easily and often. *A Slow Dance* (1975) was followed by a reclaimed *Poisoned Lands* (1976) and *The Great Cloak* (1978). What Liam had restored for poets like Kinsella and myself was the possibility of having a normal career, one volume evolving from another. But with *Selected Poems* (1982), and, more particularly, *The Dead Kingdom* (1984), I began to realize that something was wrong. Liam did not bring his old enthusiasm to planning my new books; indeed he farmed out the *Selected Poems* to my Canadian editor, Barry Callaghan. I had the impression that it was not only because he was older, but because he was distracted. Or perhaps my work was now too familiar to him: he was very excited by working with the English poet Kathleen Raine on her books of lyrics. And above all, her extraordinary study of the esoteric side of Yeats, *Yeats the Initiate*, which, with its many illustrations, must have been one of the most expensive of all the Dolmen productions. While sustaining the new poetry, Liam had always been a Yeatsian, and this opulent volume was his deepest homage to that mighty presence.

When it came to *The Dead Kingdom*, I found most of the images for the five movements myself, in sharp contrast to our exuberant collaboration on the illustrations for *The Rough Field*. He accepted them gladly, but the old gleam was gone, and when the book appeared, it had shrunk in format, as though he had to economize on paper. Only the Canadian publication, from Callaghan's Exile Editions, restored the larger dimensions that we had envisaged. And Barry, a bit of a Diaghilev himself in his efforts to warm Canada's frozen wastes, warned me that he felt my old friend Liam was 'losing it'.

Some of Liam's distractions were indeed financial. It was almost impossible then to run a small prestigious poetry press with high literary standards but little or no commercial clout. Liam was wonderful at designing a book, but when the child was delivered, he was often less interested, although arranging co-publication could still bring zest to his eye and step. We had all spent an hilarious semi-holiday at a Celtic festival in Toronto, Tom

Kinsella and myself reading, and Seán Ó Riada playing. Liam helped to produce an offbeat and ultra-modern version of Yeats's play *The Only Jealousy of Emer*, with designs by a Canadian Jewish sculptor called Sorel Etrog, who dressed Cuchulain as an American college football star, bulky shoulder pads and all. Liam published the proceedings (including a clash between myself and Conor Cruise O'Brien on the subject of the North) in a bumper volume called *The Celtic Consciousness*. I accidentally met him on Fifth Avenue after he had sold this blockbuster to a New York publisher, George Braziller, and he was high as a kite, playful as a kitten. And of course he had established a good working relationship with Oxford, Dillon Johnston's Wake Forest University Press, and sometimes Callaghan's Exile Editions. By now he was recognized as the founding father of modern Irish publishing, and he would meet his younger confrères, like Seamus Cashman of Wolfhound and Ann Tannahill of Blackstaff, for convivial evenings at the Frankfurt Book Fair.

I wonder sometimes if I played my part in his problems by not insisting on a proper author-publisher relationship; I knew little or nothing about the details of these four-way publications. It may shock people to know that I never received royalties, even for *The Rough Field*, but we operated under a kind of gentleman's agreement: he produced the Book Beautiful, and I could have as many copies as I wanted whenever I needed them. I usually had another salary from teaching, which he patently did not, so why worry? A few times I tried to work out how matters stood, but the figures varied so wildly that I gave up trying to make sense of it all. The only aspect of this haphazard bookkeeping that made me a little sore was when the Press absorbed royalties from re-publication as their due. But it is hard to dun a generous friend over money matters, and Liam had become more taciturn, so that I could not mount the rescue operation I had tried in the mid-sixties, when he was in trouble.

Besides, I had experienced, in a minor way, some of the pressures he was under. In the seventies I tried to operate a private imprint, the Golden Stone, to maintain a friendly rivalry with Kinsella's Peppercanister, and to generally keep the juices flowing in a then artistically sleepy Cork. Liam was, as ever, helpful with the planning and design, but it became clear, by the third publication, that we did not have the kind of follow-through to keep such an enterprise going. It did, however, give me a sense of how much dedication is required to keep even a minuscule imprint alive. All the tedious details of packaging and posting, lists of review and complimentary copies to journals and libraries, maintaining clear accounts, handling readers' enthusiasms and rages: it wasn't long before I lost heart. There were also local difficulties; I could not find someone to bind the special editions, and the then president of University College, Cork, decided that I was running a massive commercial operation from my office in the English Department, which was the only stable address we then had.

I was also realizing that I did not possess the publisher's temperament. It takes a certain kind of obsessive passion to corral and organize a number of writers, to encourage their gift, edit their poetry or prose, all the while keeping in sight the ideals of one's own particular publishing house. I have already mentioned Diaghilev, and indeed an impresario quality seems to be needed. At best, this quality fosters talent and creates lovely books. But it has its dark side as well, as when Dolmen felt no urgency to pay royalties, or absorbed authors' cheques into their own coffers: sometimes the imprint is seen as greater than the authors it serves.

The bond between author and publisher is rarely analyzed, yet it is an essential and often emotional relationship, especially when the material being edited and published is creative. Timothy O'Keeffe would use my arrival in London as an excuse for a lunch at the Spanish Club, drinking clubs all afternoon, and Museum Street's Plough in the evening. And although there would not be all that much direct conversation about work, it would be a consistent undercurrent. Liam was the same, and, during those hours of comradeship, there did not seem to be a mean bone in his body. He wrote to me about my part in the *Collected Poems*, saying it would re-establish Kavanagh in the race, and he echoed Behan's favourite war-cry, 'Hump the begrudgers!'

Liam Miller's end was hard. He had established a new rhythm, with the Press on the north side of Dublin and his home in a former rectory in Mountrath, his home town, with the river flowing at the end of the garden and the Goldsmithian peace of those midland fields. And yet something was wrong. He was slower and more troubled. He had a fine room that served as his office with many of his precious icons around (mainly books and engravings), and we worked there on our last project, my selected essays, a large volume of nearly three hundred pages. I remember his being particularly vehement in wishing to include many of the sleeve notes I had done for Claddagh Records, on Graves, Sidney Goodsir-Smith and of course the now neglected Ambassador Iremonger. I was never to see that manuscript again. And when I adjourned to the local, as usual, his daughter accompanied me, but Liam excused himself on grounds of tiredness.

When I next saw Liam alone, he was in Baggot

Street Hospital, and the prognosis was not good. He was trying to keep the flag flying, however, sipping whiskey as he enthused about his latest project, an edition of *Dubliners* illustrated by Louis le Brocquy, a project which would later be taken from him when he was too enfeebled to see it through. His daughter Máire was trying to run the Press, and had published some of my students, the younger Cork poets Seán Dunne and Greg Delanty, a link Liam had already forged when he published Thomas McCarthy. While I was there, a meal came, and I was impressed by the zest with which Liam tackled his grub: this was not a man resigned to illness.

All through his downward spiral, his fortitude was remarkable. Even to the last, he loved the friendly jar, but a growing despair underlay everything. Lying in a relative's home on the north side, after being discharged from hospital, he showed me the swellings on his body, and declared grimly, 'I don't think even the poet's blessing could banish these.' And yet he prayed, and believed, all the more when he was removed to a hospice in south Dublin. What characterized Liam for me, above all, was his profound Christianity. Indeed, he seems to me to have been a medieval man, in his devotion to printing as a craft, and in his faith, which was being so sorely tested. I think he was rarely as happy as when he worked with the Vatican, designing a Missal for the English-speaking world, or presenting a volume to the Pope. A photo shows Liam, lean and bearded as a medieval monk, exchanging smiles with the burly John Paul.

At his funeral, as Tom Kinsella spoke, I could not help but notice the contrast between Liam's fate and that of most of his family, who were long-lived, as the tombstone told. As the mourners scattered back to Dublin, there were many casualties: Ronnie Drew was very upset, and I was not so far behind, myself. Rumour had it that Liam had died in debt, but then, in his precarious position as a pioneer of Irish publishing, he had been moving in and out of solvency all his working life, always bouncing back — until now.

I was able to do one last service for my old friend, because I was friendly, at the time, with the librarian in charge of the Special Collections at Wake Forest University. I suggested that he should consider Liam's archive, rich with lively correspondence, and offering intriguing glimpses into the process, mechanics and day-to-day working life of a whole literary period, which he had helped to orchestrate. And of course, as I hope this testimony proves, Liam's presence is still with many of us. His wife, Josephine, described to me how, sifting through his papers and books, she had the impression of being guided, her hand opening just the right book at the right moment. Calling on his sister in Mountrath, not far from their own old home, she told me that she was sure that Liam was in heaven, and that she prayed to him. If he is, he is probably ensconced in a corner with a small printing press, and starting out all over again.

From *Company: A Chosen Life* (London: Duckworth, 2001).

DOLMEN: BOUND AND UNBOUND

RORY BRENNAN

Joyce claimed somewhere that the soul, like the body, has a virginity. The soul's virgin state is ravished by religion and the more intense forms of literature such as drama or poetry. The young Joyce, we will all remember, wanted to inscribe his precious poems on vellum and then send them off to all the great libraries, including Alexandria. This urge to encase the written text beautifully is an act of deep homage, as innumerable splendid *relieures* demonstrate (the French *relier*, to find, and religion share the same root). As a schoolboy, discovering poetry with the turbulent intensity of adolescence, I trawled the Dublin second-hand shops of forty years ago for editions, such as old Folio Society ones, whose design and feel echoed, I hoped, their rare contents. One afternoon this infant bibliomane found the slimmest of slim volumes in Hodges Figgis, then right opposite its current site in Dawson Street. This offering — 'between boards' would be the catalogue description — was a collection of *Irish Elegies* by Padraic Colum. Even as I took it down from the shelf I knew it was something special, and when I opened it and saw the title-page with its wonderful medallion portrait of Colum, I was sure. It did not matter much then, nor does it now, that the poems were, if sincere, a little lame. The book was the thing; the way it handled, the way the page sat open, the pattern of the print, all seemed to enhance the memories it contained. The imprint was Dolmen, though the famous logo does not appear. The price was seven and sixpence, the cost of a modest night out.

I was abroad when I wrote my first book in my early thirties. I thought of Dolmen as the putative publisher, the way Irish playwrights once regarded the Abbey. Liam Miller accepted the manuscript, though it must be admitted that as it arrived with the Patrick Kavanagh Award, which defrayed printing costs, this may have been an inducement above whatever other merits it may have possessed. Later, in the eighties, I became director of Poetry Ireland and quite often met Liam, mostly at book launches. Once, with John Montague, he called at our offices in Upper Mount Street, a location with its place in Dolmen lore as that of the Press's place of business. Dolmen of course issued a number of fine booklets under the imprint of Poetry Ireland Editions; so another circle was, for a time, complete. Austin Clarke's personal library stared down at us from high shelves like — to borrow John Montague's best-known line — well, like Dolmens.

In almost a decade as an arts administrator I learned the whimsical and devious ways of councils and committees. One of the responsibilities of the cultural bureaucrat is similar to that of a teacher in the classroom: to spot not merely the bright but the outstandingly gifted pupil. That Dolmen was a publishing house beyond the ordinary was, by then, abundantly apparent. But its exceptional qualities were evident virtually from the beginning. These qualities did not merely lie in the writers on the list; Dolmen's list, more than that of most publishers, varied from the glorious to the mundane. Nor does the uniqueness lie in the splendour of certain editions, of which Kinsella's *The Táin* and Montague's *The Rough Field* are perhaps the most enduring examples. Design and production too could vary. Rather the strength of Dolmen lay in its flair, in a kind of celebratory élan, in being a crucible, a vessel, an inspiring means. Nothing, perhaps, illustrates this more than the stories of famously rejected manuscripts. Whether they are folk myths of literary history or are dourly true does not really matter. What they illustrate is a profligacy, a high-handedness, a seizing of the day. There was a rakish whiff of genius about Liam Miller and the Dolmen Press.

That so much was accomplished with — and without — meagre state grants is remarkable. To return to the teacher analogy, the brilliant pupil was not spotted or, if spotted, ignored. The arts administrator has an onus to be fair, to give each little claimant a more or less equal share of the (then) skimpy booty. Dolmen suffered under this worthy if unenlightened rule. It was not like the others; if Penguin famously educated a generation, Dolmen — in Ireland — educated the taste of another. It should not have existed in a state of semi-starvation; it had long proved itself by the seventies and eighties, and if a fraction of what was spent on, say, translating state forms into Irish had been diverted to its coffers then many of its struggles would have been unnecessary. In fact, if proper support had been present the Press would have been able to nurture and sustain writers who in turn could have made it highly profitable. Instead the writer was often treated as the weakest link in the printer-to-bookseller chain. It is not fanciful to claim that Dolmen could still be with us as a truly international publishing house (to this day a great gap in the presentation of Irish writing). Instead we have high prices for old Dolmens in the dealers' catalogues. The Dolmen Press will not come again, we shall not see its like and we will not have the chance to make the same mistake.

THE DOLMEN MISCELLANY

MAURICE HARMON

In the nineteen-fifties and early sixties there were signs of fresh developments in Irish writing: slim collections by Thomas Kinsella, John Montague and Richard Murphy, novels by John McGahern, Edna O'Brien and Brian Moore, a collection of short stories by Aidan Higgins. The publication of *The Dolmen Miscellany* in September 1962 signalled the arrival of another generation. Edited by John Montague, with Thomas Kinsella as poetry editor, its two-paragraph introduction was careful not to make excessive claims. 'In recent years', it said, 'a new generation of writers has begun to emerge in Ireland, probably the most interesting since the realists of the 1930s.'

While not forming any sort of movement, they do reflect a general change of sensibility, and this Miscellany is an attempt to provide them with a platform. They are, in general, more literary than their predecessors: many of them are poets, and the prose-writers seem to be working a more experimental form of story. The main link between them, however, is their obvious desire to avoid the forms of 'Irishism' (whether leprechaun or garrulous rebel) which have been so profitably exploited in the past. In such a context, a little solemnity may be a revolutionary gesture.

We have concentrated on work of some length, or of a kind not usually represented in magazines, in the hope that, as well as providing an impetus, *The Dolmen Miscellany* will also be a record of work in progress by a generation. Future issues will, of course, depend upon your support.

(There were no further issues.)

The Dolmen Miscellany reflects and identifies a moment in the history of modern Irish literature. The contributors include Brian Moore, Aidan Higgins, John McGahern and James Plunkett, with a short story and a review by John Jordan, a critical essay on Oliver Goldsmith by John Montague and poems by Thomas Kinsella, Richard Murphy, Pearse Hutchinson, James Liddy, Richard Weber and Valentin Iremonger.

What made the *Miscellany* distinctive was its high standards. Brian Moore's 'Preliminary Pages for a Work of Revenge' is more experimental than one might have expected from the author of *Judith Hearne* and *The Feast of Lupercal*. Aidan Higgins was represented by the opening sequence of his novel, *Langrishe, Go Down*, the heightened, impressionistic description of Helen Langrishe's journey by bus from Aston Quay in Dublin to Celbridge, County Meath. John McGahern contributed his portrait of the Regan family that would appear in *The Barracks,* narrating the tensions and difficulties of the family. The quirky comedy of James Plunkett's 'Ferris Moore and the Earwig' is different in approach from his stories in *The Trusting and the Maimed.*

Thomas Kinsella's 'A Country Walk' is a formal, elegantly descriptive account of the interaction between the walker and his surroundings and within historical, mythological and contemporary contexts. Richard Murphy's 'The Cleggan Disaster' introduced a poet from an Anglo-Irish background who was deeply responsive to life in the west of Ireland. In the account of Pat Concannon's handling of the boat, reminiscent of some Anglo-Saxon poems, the poem paid restrained tribute to skill and courage. Despite his attraction to the romance of the sea, Richard Murphy was a realist intent on accurate portrayal through a quiet and measured response.

The reviews by John Montague and John Jordan are more sharply focused than the observations in the Introduction. In his discussion of recent fiction John Montague writes that the *Miscellany* was meant to be a representative cross-section and that in the process of gathering the material certain general facts about Irish writing had emerged.

Since the death of Yeats, Irish poetry had not sought nor had it received much outside interest, but with the publication of Patrick Kavanagh's *Come Dance with Kitty Stobling* and Austin Clarke's *Later Poems* that began to change. Prose, on the other hand, had enjoyed more prominence. The 'lyrical' short-story writers of the thirties had retained their popularity, but work 'outside that mould', such as the early stories of Samuel Beckett or Patrick Kavanagh's *Tarry Flynn,* had been 'relatively ignored'. But here, too, there was a change, since some recently published books suggested the appearance of 'a wider variety of approach, both in subject matter and style'. Montague praises *Felo de Se* by Aidan Higgins for its verbal wit, carefully annotated naturalist's interest in human specimens, and detached fastidiousness shading into repulsion. Flann O'Brien's *The Hard Life,* he claims, is a masterpiece in deliberately controlled stage-Irishism. He welcomes John Broderick's *The Fugitives* as the work of a Catholic novelist and likes the 'almost clinical way' in which it dramatizes 'our chief national offence, a denial of the possibilities of life in the name of a communal falsely religious death-wish'.

In his review of current collections of poetry John Jordan singles out the work of Thomas Kinsella for grace and coherence in unfolding difficult themes, delight in 'sheer texture', cool and elegant versions of romantic passion. The recent verse he finds more impersonal and more mordant. 'Old Harry', the poem about President Harry Truman's decision to drop the atomic bomb, may, he says, be the best poem in English about this event; *Poems and Translations* has 'authority and the excitement of measured growth'. Whereas Kinsella's poetry, Jordan notes, did not have much in it that was specifically Irish, John Montague's did. Montague is interested in the truth of landscape and object and the fable-value of disparate fragments of erudition. It is significant, in view of the remark about 'Irishisms', that Jordan finds it necessary to point out that Irish themes are not aesthetically or morally unjustifiable.

The *Miscellany* reflected what was happening in fiction, poetry and criticism. By the variety and high standard of its contributions it signalled that indeed an important new generation was in the process of being created. Irish writers came out of the long shadows of Yeats and Joyce, expressing a different Ireland from that of O'Faolain and Austin Clarke. They were part not only of a post-Civil War mentality but of a post-World War II consciousness and did not want to be identified on the basis of 'Irishisms'. They looked outward whereas the generation that preceded them tended to look inward. As time passed they manifested a dual vision, outward-looking for ideas, for awareness of literary developments, inward-looking for a deeper exploration of their cultural and linguistic origins. The very notion of being an Irish writer underwent change. Whereas the generation of the thirties had been immersed in nationalistic ideals, many of them directly involved in revolutionary activity, these writers had a cooler, more detached response. The kind of ready response to nationalistic feelings that characterized O'Faolain, O'Connor and Clarke, who identified with the upsurge of rebellious feelings and had a later recoil from it, was replaced in Kinsella by a deeper psychological process in which the understanding of self was related to an understanding of a past that originated in pre-history. It was perhaps their imaginative freedom that most distinguished the new writers and their successors, an ability to roam freely for subject matter and setting, to draw at will from traditions and achievements wherever they found them, to be experimental, if it suited them, to be first and foremost writers, rather than be self-consciously or defensively Irish writers. Since then Irish literature has confirmed what was stated in the *Miscellany*'s introduction: a new generation did emerge and the note of confidence was justified.

For those who were watching the signs of a possible reawakening, acquiring each slim volume as a token of what might follow, the appearance of *The Dolmen Miscellany* was a quiet manifesto. I had my copy sent by Michael Freyer from the Brown Jacket Bookshop in Lower Baggot Street, together with Austin Clarke's *Forget Me Not,* a Dolmen catalogue and a note from Michael to say that Clarke's plays would follow. As I look at the invoice I notice that it is addressed to 'Maurice Harmon, Esq.'. Style added to substance.

Tucked into the volume I find reviews from *The Irish Times*: Bruce Arnold's perceptive response to McGahern's *The Barracks,* Margaret Stanley-Wrench's identification of the voice of a 'real poet' in Richard Murphy's *Sailing to an Island,* and Terence de Vere White's appropriately serious response to the seriousness of tone in *The Dolmen Miscellany*. Looking at these scraps now it seems remarkable how quickly the new generation developed. Ten years earlier, Irish writing had been almost invisible. Now it was sturdily present.

BORGES, BECKETT AND THE ROME MATRICES

Bernard Share

Bernardo's Restaurant, Dublin, sometime in the late autumn of 1970. Over a modest lunch, Liam Miller and Michael Gill are interviewing me for the part-time post of secretary of the newly formed Irish Book Publishers' Association, subsequently to be rechristened Clé (Cumannleabhar-fhoil-sitheoirí Éireann) by the formidable Bríd Bean Uí hÉeagartaigh of Sáirséal & Dill. Publishing at the time was only beginning to re-emerge, thanks very largely to the energy, enterprise and vision of Miller, as a serious native endeavour and it was something, I convinced myself, that I would like to be part of. Not that I did not experience certain reservations about trying to sit on the solid fence dividing writer and publisher with a leg dangling on each side.

My first contact with Liam Miller dated from

1954, when, with a handful of published poems to my credit, I came across the Dolmen Press in the form of an elegantly printed announcement that it was proposing to produce 'a series of books of new verse and invites manuscript material for consideration ...'. This appeared over the address '8 Sion Hill Road, Drumcondra, Dublin, Ireland' — Miller was thinking internationally even then. Publication of the six proposed volumes was planned for autumn 1954, but it was well into that season (or rather it was summer, for I had in the meantime embarked upon the seven-week voyage to Australia) before I heard anything further. A letter in Miller's distinctive hand, dated 1 November 1954, but emanating now from the new address at 111 Silchester Park, Glenageary, informed me that my work would not be featured in the first six editions, 'but, should the initial series succeed and a second becomes possible we hope that you will again allow us to consider your work for inclusion'. But by now, caught up as I was in the complexities of a strange land, both Dublin and Dolmen seemed very far away, and both faded into the distance along with my still-born poetic début.

Some sixteen years later the new encounter with Miller was to evolve into a working relationship which brought me into close contact with the key attributes of this many-faceted man. Under the auspices of Córas Tráchtála, the export board, the fledgling publishers' group made several sallies, in the company of a posse of book printers, to New York in an endeavour to promote Irish books in that market. I tagged along as both secretary and general dogsbody, and it was in this latter capacity that I was enabled to see Miller in action in areas which lay close to his credo as both publisher and printer. On one of these trips in the early 1970s I found myself invited to accompany him to a meeting with the Argentinian writer Jorge Luis Borges. Miller moved in mysterious ways, and I was unclear as to both the purpose of the visit and my function in the matter — unless it was to act as translator of Borges's Spanish. In the event this proved to be totally unnecessary, his English being excellent, but he was virtually blind and probably was as confused by the brief encounter as was I. What emerged, of course, was the magnificent volume of *Irish Strategies*, signed by Borges, translator Anthony Kerrigan and illustrator Bernard Childs, published in January 1976.

My secretarial and adjunctive duties took me every year to the Frankfurt Buchmesse — no place for a writer, practising or aspiring — and it was on the way back from one such function in the 1970s that I found myself with Miller in Paris. My purpose was to meet an old friend of mine, an Australian historian; Miller's, as I was to discover, to try to track down the elusive matrices of a fount of Irish type used in the printing works of the Rome Propaganda in 1676 and allegedly 'souvenired' by Napoleon and brought back to Paris. The background to this quest is too complex to go into here, but Colm Ó Lochlainn had been on the same mission to the Imprimerie Nationale in 1936 and Miller was to be followed in 1987 by Dermot McGuinne, as recorded in his *Irish Type Design* (1992). On this occasion I was enlisted, quite positively this time, as Miller's translator, facility in languages not being among his endowments. My French was passable, but as we climbed the stairs I began wondering what was the equivalent in that language of 'X-height' or 'beard', let alone 'Nonpareil' ('Nompril' in printers' Dublinese). Flanked by my Australian friend, who had come along for the ride but whose interest in typography was as minimal as his understanding of French, I did solitary battle, but to little avail. I cannot recollect now what exactly Miller discovered, if anything — but it was certainly not the fate of the missing matrices. There was no questioning, however, either his typographical knowledge or his anxiety to pursue this recondite enquiry to a successful conclusion.

A more fruitful Parisian endeavour, again on the way back from Frankfurt, was one in which I counted myself privileged to be involved. Miller had persuaded Samuel Beckett to allow him to reprint his translation of *Zone*, by Guillaume Apollinaire, which had originally appeared in the avant-garde magazine *transition*; though Miller was to state in *Dolmen XXV* that 'Samuel Beckett's interest in our work led him to offer us *Zone*'. Whatever the origin of the initial impetus, Beckett had generously agreed to sign 250 copies of the limited edition. So in the autumn of 1971, after a series of phone calls to Beckett's very private number, we were invited to present ourselves at his equally anonymous apartment near the Boulevard Montmartre. Whether Miller had enlisted my company out of the goodness of his heart or simply because 250 books in sheets was rather a load to carry I am still unsure, but we rang the bell and Beckett's voice told us to come in and take the lift.

What followed was something that Sam might have scripted: the street door closed behind us, leaving us in total darkness. Failing to locate the *minuterie* we groped our way to the lift, only to find that conveyance in total darkness too and reluctant to ascend. Inevitably, we pressed the wrong button and were slowly translated, still in pitch darkness, to the very top of the building. When we did eventually arrive, blinking, at the right floor after an unplanned stygian return to ground level, a somewhat amused Beckett was waiting for us. The bottle of Jameson we had brought together with the pile of unbound pages died a leisurely death.

For me such incidents, if of minor significance individually, taken together characterized Liam Miller's determination to work, from a very small base, within both a global and a national framework; and to work, in terms both of authors and of typography and book production, to the highest standards. Nowadays copies of his Borges and Beckett which appear in booksellers' catalogues are invariably followed by the description 'rare'. It is a not inappropriate categorization of the man and his achievement.

ANTIQUARIAN AND ARCHIVAL ICONS

The Graphic Ornamentation of John Montague's The Rough Field *(1972) and* The Dead Kingdom *(1984)*

Thomas Dillon Redshaw

The solid rectangularity of John Montague's *Collected Poems* (Gallery Press, 1995) houses much of his work newly re-orchestrated, as the publisher's afterword notes. The book opens with new settings of *The Rough Field* (1972), *The Great Cloak* (1978), and *The Dead Kingdom* (1984), all originally published by Liam Miller's Dolmen Press, which also issued Montague's *Selected Poems* (1982). A very comprehensive selection, this earlier volume closes with a re-orchestration of *A Slow Dance* (1975) with the three titles already mentioned, the title of *The Dead Kingdom* lacking a date. The poems in Montague's *Selected* lack iconic decoration, though the first half opens with Louis le Brocquy's cover drawing for *A Chosen Light* (1967) and the second half opens with John

Derricke's Elizabethan woodblock of the dancing bard and closes with the seal of the United Irishmen — both icons first employed by Liam Miller in his setting of Montague's *Patriotic Suite* (1966). In contrast, the 376 pages of the *Collected* offer the reader no sense of the poems' heritage of emblems, and by design, for the book expresses the design conventions favoured by Peter Fallon and Dillon Johnston. There, in those opening pages, *The Rough Field* and *The Dead Kingdom* appear as words, epigrams, lyrics, and strophes alone.

The Dead Kingdom appeared from the Dolmen Press after Liam Miller had moved to Mountrath, a few years before his death. The new sequence was published with what Miller counted as the fourth edition of Montague's *The Rough Field* (1972). Both books were designed by Miller; they were conceived as a pair and issued as trade publications, almost as 'pocket editions' — as near to mass-market books as collections of poems can come. Unfortunately, both were printed on inexpensive paper having a high acid content and, thus, both books display an alarming tendency to yellow rapidly. Both have the same dimensions (19.5 cm by 12.75 cm). *The Rough Field* has a greeny-gold cover and bears John Derricke's figure of the harper under the title; *The Dead Kingdom* has a violet-grey cover and bears a high-contrast photograph of a fetish from Boa Island, County

Fermanagh, on the cover. Clearly, and with Montague's approval, Miller designed the books as a contrastive pair, and that contrast of emblematic vocabularies may have its own significance.

Miller's fourth edition of *The Rough Field* merely repeats in smaller format the design of the original and gives it the least inspired cover of all the book's editions. It preserves the original's lexicon of decoration, of visual epigraphs, drawn from Small's 1883 facsimile edition of John Derricke's *The Image of Irelande* with *A Discourie of Woodkarne*. Derricke's 'Notable Discouery' occupies a calendar of twelve wood-block plates, and these Liam Miller exploited so assiduously in the service of Montague's poetry that quotations of Derricke's propagandizing illustrations became, somewhat ironically, one of the hallmarks of the Dolmen style — the other being the brushwork of Louis le Brocquy associated with Thomas Kinsella's *The Táin* (1969).

Of course, the Dolmen Press displayed the talents of many artists and typographers in Ireland during its thirty-five years, and Miller lists them fondly in his introduction to *Dolmen XXV* (1976). The study of architecture formed Miller's tastes, and Dolmen's vocabulary of design during its first decade owed much less to the precedent of the Yeats sisters and the Cuala Press than to the English example set by Eric Gill and René Hague in the 1930s. Elizabeth Rivers's decorations as well as Michael Biggs's letter-cutting, for instance, reflect the ethos of design advocated in the work of the Golden Cockerell Press and Hague and Gill in the 1920s and 1930s. In the 1960s, as the Dolmen Press came to be the representative Irish 'art' publisher, Miller chose to mark the centenary of the birth of W.B. Yeats with the twelve fascicles of the *Yeats Centenary Papers* (1965–68) and the half-centenary of the Easter Rising with *Patriotic Suite*

(November 1966). This was the first of 'The New Dolmen Chapbooks'. Thomas Kinsella had presided over the twelve parts of the first *Dolmen Chapbook* (1954–60). Miller described *Patriotic Suite* as having been published 'With reproductions of old cuts', but it contains one new 'cut' — the chapbook emblem graven in Gill's manner by Tate Adams.

Patriotic Suite in both its trade and collector's editions offers the reader three 'old cuts': the closing seal of the United Irishmen and two from plates illustrating the 'state and condition of the Wild men in Ireland' rising against the Pale and at length submitting to Sir Henry Sidney in 1578. The cover cut for *Patriotic Suite* shows: 'Here creepes out of *Sainct Filchers denne*, a pack of prowling mates, / Most hurtfull to the English pale ...'. The war-piper is followed by swordsmen and infantry bearing halberds. Miller left out the rest of Derricke's plate, in which, to the right, pikemen burn a house on the edge of the Pale, and at the top other infantry drive cattle away — along with an English tenant on horseback. The title-page bears an old cut from Derricke's third plate, displaying the feast of Mac Sweynes, O'Neill's gallowglasses, after a cattle raid on the Pale. This version appears as the cover of the 1989 Bloodaxe and Wake Forest printings of *The Rough Field*. And from this plate Miller selected the archetypal figure of the harper seated at the bottom right of the plate: 'Both Barde, and Harper, is preparde, which by their cunning art, / Doe strike and cheare up all the gestes, with comfort at the hart'. That figure of the harper decorates the cover of the 1984 edition of *The Rough Field,* while the figure of the 'barde', really a *reacaire* or 'reciter', heads the title-page.

Derricke's figure of the 'barde' occurs on the title-pages of all editions of *The Rough Field* except those last issued in 1989 by the Gallery Press and Bloodaxe Books.

The first edition's brown cover excerpts the scene from Plate II of the house-burning, as does the second, though the third departs from Derricke's visual diction by reproducing the seal of the United Irishmen on an orange field.

Moreover, as Montague's readers know, all ten cantos of *The Rough Field* open with icons drawn from Derricke's plates — but not quite all. The decoration for Canto X, 'The Wild Dog Rose', derives from the verdure sheltering John Derricke's initials ('ID') under the feet of 'Donolle obreane, the messenger', in Plate VII, to whom Sir Henry is giving a letter of 'peace' to deliver to The O'Neill. But Miller's version leaves out the messenger, Sir Henry bending down from his steed, and the pikemen ranked on either side. Instead, he has drawn in the '*wild dog rose*', *rosa rugosa,* as if to echo the Tudor rose, and the peace that the 'honour of that Queene' prefers. The image is Miller's, not Derricke's.

So, *The Rough Field*'s lexicon of visual decoration may, in the main, be traced back to Miller's percipient and contrastive selection of Derricke's imagery in the 1966 setting of *Patriotic Suite*. There is clear evidence, though, that Miller thought to provide *The Rough Field*'s cantos with an entirely different vocabulary of emblems. In 1972 the Irish Book Publishers' Association published *Sampla,* an anthology of sample typography and design by thirteen Irish book houses. Dolmen contributed *The Rough Field*'s first canto, 'Home Again', decorated with an ink drawing of 'Dagda's Cauldron', a Bronze Age Celtic artifact recently unearthed in Monaghan. It is likely that Miller executed the drawing himself, from archaeological photographs, before June 1971. A larger rendition of the cauldron appears on a 'specimen' printing of the cantos dated June 1971. This suggests that, had his energies not been distracted by the business of publishing, Miller might have created a complete set of drawings for the poem and, thus, a very different and differently evocative vocabulary of emblems.

But, after many meetings with Montague, Miller returned to the precedent of *Patriotic Suite*. Montague's sequence is dedicated to the composer Seán Ó Riada, who composed the film music for a trio of documentary films funded by Gael Linn: *Mise Éire* (1959), *Saoirse* (1960), *An Tine Bheo* (1966). In the first film, Ó Riada orchestrates variations on 'Róisín Dubh' to go with documentary footage of the Easter Rising edited by George Morrison. Accordingly, Miller set the cut of Derricke's 'pyper' leading the kerne — a figure killed off in Plate IX — on the cover and at the head of *Patriotic Suite*. Montague's 'suite' of poems steals some effects from American Modernism and others from Austin Clarke's curmudgeonly satire of the 1950s. Each movement in the suite satirizes the failure of the Rising with atmospheric variations on the historical ironies created by raised expectations, as in 'Build-Up':

Elegant port-wine brick, a colonial dream:
Now we own the cow, why keep the cream?

While Montague's poems here form little more than a narrative of scornful disappointments, the narrative of the Rising itself was one of immediate failure, and the narrative of Derricke's propagandizing plates is that of eventual 'comming in of *Thirlaugh Leonaugh* the great **Oneale** of Ireland submitting himselfe to the right honorable *Syr Henry Sydney*'.

In all editions of *The Rough Field* (1972–1989), *Patriotic Suite* opens with the same 'old cut' from Derricke. Indeed, Miller raided Derricke's plates shamelessly, and in picking images from Derricke's pictorial narrative he let the topical force of Montague's lines, poems, and cantos determine the choice of icon in terms of direct correspondence. For instance, canto four, 'A Severed Head', opens not only with quotations from Sir John Davies and George Hill, but also with the image in Derricke's fifth plate of Sidney's men leading the troops back with two swordsmen holding Irish heads high like olives on toothpicks and a musketeer gripping a bleeding head by the glib. Here the images stolen from Derricke's Elizabethan narrative of a failed rising — of Irish submission and of English dominance — have been reordered according to cues raised by the distant and ultimately autobiographical effects of that rising in the central persona of *The Rough Field*. It is not entirely clear whether the modern autobiographical narrative of Mac an Teigue, the poet, succeeds in subverting the fragments Derricke's antique triumph of Sir Henry Sidney, the father of Sir Philip the poet.

The cantos of *The Dead Kingdom* document and enact another failure to return, a journey north to the purlieux of Fintona, the Sperrin hills, and County Tyrone — and to the burials of his aunt and foster-mother Winifred Montague and his mother Mary (or 'Molly') Carney. Montague orchestrates the phases of his return into five cantos. Each is tagged with epigraphs. The whole poem starts with a line from Pablo Neruda, and the cantos follow with epigraphs in prose and verse, with sources and without, from religion (*The Epic of Gilgamesh*), from world literature (Kafka, Beckett, Hesse), from Tyrone folksong and Cork pub-talk, from poetry and pop song (Johns Donne and Lennon). And the frame of allusion tends to shift from the archetypal to the typical, as if to incarnate the particular biography, the particular mourning of the poems with the universal, as if to assert the momentary inhabitation of the particular by the eternal. Likewise, from cover to last canto, *The Dead Kingdom*'s essentially photographic decorations have a similar framing effect on the suites of poems in the collection.

As noted before, *The Dead Kingdom*'s cover offers a high-contrast photograph of a sixth-century carving found on Boa Island, a head fetish related to the Horned God cult of northern Celtic culture of the La Tène period — a figure that identifies the poet and persona of the poems and echoes the autobiographical *tête coupée* motifs in *The Rough Field*. Answering or challenging that in a thoroughly Oedipal manner is the larger photographic image on the half-title page. The image seems both to represent and to cause overexposure. This, of course, is the legendary Sheelah-na-Gig (*Síle na gCíoch*) beloved by aficionados of Gravesian muse-worship. The National Gallery has this piece in captivity in the Dawson Collection. It was taken from the Old Church in Cavan town. Myth critics offer parallel identifications of the figure: it is Babd or Baubo, the Personified Yoni, the Divine Hag, or the Heraldic Woman.

Here, in such a position, that figure's meanings serve as premises for the agonies of mourning that the poems of *The Dead Kingdom* enact. Canto I, 'Upstream', offers a clearer but smaller and less potent photographic emblem: a tomb model of a Nile boat meant to stand concretely for the transportation of the dead soul up the River of Life. This object, like the one following, can be seen in the British Museum. For Canto II, 'This Neutral Realm', Miller's setting offers a starker and bigger emblem, but one from an actual Viking ship sunk in the river Scheldt and not the Nile model. The prow is four feet, nine inches tall in actuality, and the dragon finial aptly terminates in a depiction of fierce finality. Threat is the motive, as may be said of the photographic emblem for Canto III, 'The Black Pig'. Montague's title there alludes to Irish mythology, but the object is Gaulish and was found at Neuvy-en-Sullias in Loiret. Though large (over two feet tall), this bronze is entirely typical of Celtic metalwork, and the image is entirely conventional and figures in continental Celtic lore.

The closing two cantos of *The Dead Kingdom* come prefaced by epigraphs explicitly framing the never-concluded family romance at the heart of Montague's mourning sequences. Canto V, 'A Flowering Absence', begins after John Lennon's lines: 'Mother, you had me but I never had you, / I wanted you but you didn't want me'. The epigraph follows a selection from a newspaper illustration, perhaps from Walt Whitman's Brooklyn *Eagle* — a steel engraving depicting the Brooklyn Bridge on its opening day. It is a 'real' image, a documentary image, but it also provides a symbol already defined by American popular culture and by Hart Crane. Despite its festivity, the symbol bridges past with present mourning, the sorrow of loss with the sorrow of abandonment, the unassuaged infantile trauma at the heart of the adult family romance. Preceding that comes 'The Silver Flask', Canto IV, and its epigraphic assertion of the same trauma:

> FIRST CUSTOMER: My mother?
> My mother was the
> real woman in my life. Every night I pray to
> her.

and:

> I never haid a mammy
> she soon gave me up
> I never haid a daddy
> he was always on the sup … (*TDK 58*)

These follow a photograph probably printed Victorian-style from a glass negative, for dimly in the upper left corner can be seen 'Co. Tyrone' scratched in the negative by the photographer. This is a 'real' image, a document. The man and woman posed stiffly against the *trompe-l'oeil* studio set are the parents. Though uncertain, the date can be no later than 1924 or 1925, when James Montague left Tyrone for Brooklyn owing to his Republican partisanship at the close of the Irish Civil War. Apparently mounted on a stiff card, the photograph seems something like a saint's card, something like a mass card. Though historically bound, the wedding photograph and the steel engraving have been posed to assume archetypal status that is the equal of the prior images and icons. The myths of history create the characteristic sacrifices of individuals.

Montague's published collections draw on two design traditions. Starting with the political ironies of *Patriotic Suite* (1966), Liam Miller exploited the resources of Derricke's sixteenth-century visual narrative depicting Sir Henry Sidney's triumphal command of Elizabethan Ireland from Dublin Castle. And Irish presses other than Dolmen followed suit, as may be seen in the example of the Arts Council of Northern Ireland's *Planter and Gael* souvenir programme of 1970. In contrast, the Dolmen setting of *The Dead Kingdom* exploited photographs of objects assumed to have archetypal significance in the more fundamental narrative of human consciousness. Choosing these emblems to 'lead' the stages of the persona's mourning journey seems an obviously encyclopaedic tactic.

Three families of graphic ornament have accompanied the publication of *The Rough Field* and *The Dead Kingdom*, and these have influenced the visual reception of Montague's poetry from 1967 through 1989. These are the Antiquarian or Elizabethan, the Archival, and the Abstract. Joanne Dus-Zastrow's 1989 Bolt Court Press setting of *This Neutral Realm* offers a prime example of abstract ornament. The first and most dominant family is, ironically, the Elizabethan. Its antiquarian romance proved attractive to Liam Miller's eye not so much because his model of design was the work of Eric Gill and his heirs, nor because he espoused layered ironies latent in English representations of the quaint Irish from the age of Elizabeth onwards, nor even because these decorations bore a family resemblance to the typographic traditions represented by the Yeats sisters and their Cuala Press or by the Salkelds and their Gayfield Press editions. Rather, perhaps Miller saw in the crudeness of Derricke's imagery a counter to canons of ornament and design then dominant in England in the idiom of Eric Ravilious, John Luke, or Rowel Friers dating from the late 1940s. Dolmen printings of the 1950s and early 1960s present ornament in that tradition by, for example, Tate Adams, Michael Biggs, Mia Cranwell, and Elizabeth Rivers, among others. Miller's choice of the Elizabethan or the Antiquarian idiom based on borrowings from Derricke came to be a hallmark of 'the Dolmen style'. Likewise, it came to define Montague as a poet in a narrow, if interestingly ironic manner. Unfortunately, of the three families of graphic ornament that Montague's printers have deployed on the page with his lines, poems, and cantos, the Elizabethan seems to dominate, and Montague's reader sometimes must strain through that dominance to see the poem and hear it aright.

Less frequently have Montague's poems been ornamented in the Archival mode, largely in limited, boxed editions coming from the Dolmen Press. The chief exemplar of this lexicon is *The Dead Kingdom* in the 1984 edition. The decorations — scrapbook clippings, old photos — to this edition reinforce the reader's perception of Montague as an essentially autobiographical poet, and one who sees that story in both confessionally or genealogically specific and mythic terms. This perception has confirmed the impatience of some readers with Montague's familial sorrows, and that impatience can diminish the genuine stature of some of Montague's repeated themes — emigration and binationality, fosterage and abandonment. Such an impatience may impoverish the poems, many of which are more independent of their autobiographical anchorings than strophes from Allen Ginsberg, dream songs from John Berryman, or love letters from Ted Hughes.

A longer version of this article that considered alternative designs — in particular the Joanne Dus-Zastrow setting of *This Neutral Realm* (1989) — appeared in *The South Carolina Review*, Fall 1999.

THE FINAL CHAPTER

Raymond and Nuala Gunn

RAYMOND: On Sunday, 17 May 1987 at 1.00 p.m. I heard Emer O'Kelly read the news item that Liam Miller, founder of the Dolmen Press, had died.

While it came as a shock, it did not come as a surprise, because we had, over the previous six months or so, during his illness, visited him on many occasions in Baggot Street Hospital, St Anne's Hospital in Northbrook Road, and finally, in Our Lady's Hospice in Harold's Cross, and had hoped he might recover. Unfortunately it was not to be. I broke the news to Nuala.

NUALA: I rang the Hospice and asked if it would be possible to see him in repose. They said that it would be all right to come. We went to the Hospice that afternoon. He was laid out splendidly in a beautiful suit, shirt and tie. He looked as though he were sleeping, and I thought as I looked at him that he could have been the High King of Ireland.

RAYMOND: A previous visit on Holy Saturday, which was, coincidentally, the day of the Grand National at Aintree was somewhat bizarre. While on the one hand we were watching a horse-race on a television set at Liam's bedside, we were also watching mass on a closed-circuit television system from within the chapel of the Hospice. But, in addition, we were doing something else.

NUALA: At Liam's request, we had brought with us a guitar amplifier and a small electronic keyboard. We were conducting a sing-song in his room. Liam and I sang, 'La Golondrina' and other songs in the company of some of his family, and at the request of his grandchildren, I sang a popular song by the Swedish group ABBA, 'I Have a Dream'. That was our final visit.

After the funeral service in the Hospice and during the long, slow, drive to the graveyard near Mountrath, we had time to reflect, and recall when, and how, we had first met Liam.

RAYMOND: My first introduction to Liam was in connection with a forthcoming book that he wished to have typeset. This was *Under the Moorish Wall* by Peter Luke. He sent the marked-up manuscript in the post, and so began our relationship with the Dolmen Press and Liam Miller.

NUALA: I enjoyed typesetting this book. It was beautifully written. It was as if I was transported to Andalusia, and I could almost smell the lemon-groves. Curiously, it was never published by Dolmen. Liam sold it on to some other publisher.

The next book we did for Liam was *Two Death Tales* by Maria Tymoczko.

RAYMOND: Liam's design for *Two Death Tales* was rather complicated and involved a lot of juggling with pieces of text, graphics, raised footnotes, dropped capitals, all of which had to be prepared by hand. Every page of this book was finished individually. The typesetting technology we were using at that time did not have any memory facility. Each page had to be brought to a conclusion and ready to print. Any alterations, later, would cost much time and money.

NUALA: I typeset this book on the IBM Electronic Composer, 'The Roadrunner', which in its time was an excellent machine. However, the method by which the raised footnotes, italics, accents and fadas were achieved was very slow. It involved a font change every time any of these occurred, and there were hundreds of them. But the end result was pleasing, and something to look back upon with some pride and satisfaction. It is still, for us, a pleasure to hold this book and remember.

RAYMOND: In 1982 the IBM system, which had served us so well, had now run its course and had to be replaced. Following discussions with Liam, and a series of enquiries, we bought the 'CRTronic', which was manufactured by Linotype, a renowned and historic company in terms of typesetting equipment, typefaces and typography.

At Liam's request we bought typefaces suited to his books — Garamond, Palatino and Pilgrim, which we subsquently used for the 'Peppercanister' series. The first book we did for Liam with the new system was *Immediate Man* (1983), a tribute to Cearbhall Ó Dálaigh, who had died in 1978. It was edited by Aidan Carl Mathews.

NUALA: The new equipment enabled us to recreate a facsimile of what was formerly produced in 'hot metal'. It was, in fact, a computerized version of the old hot metal. Perhaps it was even better, in that each character was absolutely perfect. The 'CRTronic' could produce anything up to 72 point, just as in the days of hot metal.

On one occasion when collecting the proofs for this book, Liam sat in an armchair in our main living-room and read through the final corrections. He was wearing a beautiful navy coat and was on his way to Áras an Uachtaráin to meet President Hillery to discuss that forthcoming publication.

I am a cat lover, and at the time I think there

might have been something like twelve cats in residence. When Liam stood up to leave I could see that his coat was covered in white cat hairs. A damage-limitation exercise had to be deployed. It took about fifteen minutes' work with adhesive tape and damp cloths to remove the cat hairs from his coat before he departed for the Áras.

RAYMOND: The next book we did with Dolmen was *The Dead Kingdom* by John Montague. Liam's design for this was simple but impressive. It was a book of poems to which he applied a style I am sure he must have used on many previous occasions. Each section had an opening page which started with a Roman numeral, followed by the title of the section, and an appropriate illustration.

NUALA: In November 1984 Liam invited us to his home in Mountrath to discuss the forthcoming publication of *Yeats the Initiate* by Kathleen Raine. Upon our arrival in Mountrath we were warmly welcomed by Liam and Jo, who kindly provided a delicious meal together with wine and convivial conversation.

RAYMOND: After the meal, Liam and I went to his study to discuss the mammoth tome that was *Yeats the Initiate*. Liam must have worked on it for a long time. He had every page planned.

Photocopies of every image were stuck to each page of the manuscript. All the illustrations were identified as to where they should appear on each page. Every enlargement and reduction was defined in percentages. Needless to say they were all absolutely accurate. I followed his instructions to the letter and they all fitted perfectly.

Pursuant to many discussions with Liam, I was eager to include the small-caps, the old-style hanging numerals and other design features that would enhance the appearance of the book. The new equipment was tailor-made for this.

NUALA: It was the largest book we had ever undertaken up to that time. During many discussions I had with Liam during the typesetting, he told me Kathleen Raine used to communicate with Yeats at night. Apparently she spoke to him in her dreams!

I recall being under considerable pressure with various deadlines that we had to meet for other clients at that time. In addition, we had recently moved house. So, on one occasion when Liam called early one morning to collect a set of proofs of *Yeats the Initiate,* I had neither completed the proofs nor had time to purchase the usual groceries. I tried to fob him off by offering him a cup of coffee and some biscuits. These so-called 'biscuits' were 'Wagon Wheels', which I had never bought before. Imagine my embarrassment when

I opened the package in his presence to discover they were huge, about four inches in diameter. He graciously took one, and accepted my promise that I would courier the proofs to him by the end of the week. Liam never applied pressure other than in a gentle and subtle way. This always worked, and the deadlines were always met.

RAYMOND: *The Irish Hand* by Timothy O'Neill was the next book we prepared for Dolmen. It was an anthology of Irish calligraphy over ten centuries. Once again Liam had spent a lot of time designing this book. There were reproductions of various manuscripts and pieces of calligraphy.

Prior to sending the manuscript, he had sent to me all of the 10″ x 8″ glossy photographs scaled to the exact size, as they would appear in the book. Later, Liam and I were disappointed upon reading a review in *Books Ireland* that was critical of the quality of the photographic reproductions of the manuscripts. The various vellum pages were reproduced from black-and-white photographs only. Perhaps they should have been in colour like the one on the front cover of the book. However, this would have involved the four-colour printing process, which was, and still is, very expensive.

NUALA: Among the last books we did for Dolmen were *Songs of the Psyche* and *Her Vertical Smile* by

Thomas Kinsella. Although these two books were quite short, 48 pages and 32 pages respectively, they took quite some time to complete.

Liam, in collaboration with Thomas Kinsella and ourselves, put a lot of time and effort into achieving the final product. The cover images, title-pages and the overall design of these books were all carefully shaped by Liam.

RAYMOND: On many occasions I asked Liam simple questions about typefaces, typography and design. His answers always provided a vast amount of information which I was only too delighted to absorb. I learnt a great deal from him.

NUALA: Working with Liam was a pleasure and a wonderful education in the area of typography and design. I shall remember him always, with great affection and fondness.

GO, LITTLE BOOK

JOHN V. KELLEHER

[John V. Kelleher's *Too Small for Stove Wood, Too Big for Kindling: Collected Verse and Translations* was published by the Dolmen Press in 1979. What follows is taken from a letter to the editor of the present book, dated 17 April 2001.—Ed.]

I think I met Liam Miller at Jack Sweeney's apartment on Beacon Street when Miller was visiting Boston. Jack had mentioned my translations to him, and Miller asked to see them and any original verse I might have committed. So I sent him a typescript of what I had. A long time passed and then quite unexpectedly I got a letter saying — if I recollect aright — that unfortunately the Dolmen had gone bankrupt and that, at least for the foreseeable future, publication of the poems was unlikely, but that things might well change …

About that time I was invited to Cornell for a term as a Fellow (I now forget exactly of what, though I remember that the offices were in the Andrew D. White house, the home of Cornell's first president, and the head of the programme, Henry Guerlac, had been a Junior Fellow at Harvard just before my time). While I was there I got another letter from Liam enclosing the proofs of the poems for me to read and correct. Naturally I did that and sent them back at once. I gathered that the Press had recovered from bankruptcy. Then another silence. Then another letter saying that the Press had gone bankrupt again, but, as proof of sincerity (which I never questioned or doubted), enclosing a sample dust jacket for the book. Sometime later I heard, I think from Jack Sweeney, that Liam had died.

Naturally I thought that was the end of the likelihood that the book would ever be published. I was very grateful to Liam for his willingness to take a chance on such a disunified collection of verse reflecting one man's somewhat improbable range of interests, and I couldn't imagine an American publisher who would have been willing to take the risk with no even moderately likely audience in prospect. Indeed if Liam had offered to publish only the translations I would have understood and have accepted without question.

So that was that. Except that after another long pause I got another letter from a man who was dealing with the remains of the Dolmen, saying that he had come across the author's copies which for some reason had been overlooked and that he was sending them along. They duly arrived and I was able to get several more from booksellers, enough to give to my sisters, daughters, and several particular friends. I also saw one brief review in an Irish paper. And every once in a while I used to get a cheque from RTÉ for readings of 'The Snoring Bedmate' on some programme, but that ceased long ago.

By the way, before I met Liam I had also given a typescript of the poems and translations to Robert Frost. We had known each other since we met at the funeral of a mutual friend, Sidney Cox, at Dartmouth. We had more than that in common: we were both from Lawrence, Massachusetts, both graduates of Lawrence High School, both friends and admirers of Constantine P. Curran, to whom AE had introduced Frost when he had visited Dublin in the 1920s. And I can add that we were both — Frost and I — warm admirers of Frost's poetry. I thought he might find some of the translations interesting and possibly one or two of the poems set in New England, but in fact he never mentioned the typescript to me though we continued very friendly. And I was not surprised. Another poet friend of mine told me quite honestly that he himself thought that he really didn't care for any poetry except his own, and I had gathered that Frost was of like mind. And of course this didn't bother me. I never thought that my stuff rated anything better than 'Not bad for a professor'.

One last detail. A young woman who got her doctorate in Celtic at Harvard and was offering a course in Early Irish Literature at Boston College had come across one of the translations and found them just what she was looking for, in contrast to the standard scholarly rephrasings. She went to Widener for the book and found that the only copy had been stolen. So she appealed to me, and I sent her a set of the proofs Liam Miller had sent me long ago. From these several new copies were made for her, for the library, and one for me. So I now have a hardback volume of my own verse.

THE DOLMEN PRESS

Thomas Kinsella

1 *Introducing: Irish Publishing*

Samuel Beckett had a mixed publishing history, due partly to his adopted exile and partly to the nature of his work. His career was established outside Ireland. Joyce's case was similar, but this was not altogether a matter of choice or neglect on his part. He tried very hard to have *Dubliners* published in Dublin. Maunsel had published books by Synge and Yeats. They finally refused Joyce.

Yeats's experience was more orderly. After early publication with Maunsel, he developed a private form of publication with the Dun Emer Press, and continued this into his mature career with the Cuala Press. A permanent professional relationship was established with Macmillan in London. Maunsel had disappeared, but its survival would have made no difference: it was not an adequate professional publisher. There was no publisher of the kind in Ireland.

But this is not the reason Yeats looked to London. Things worked the other way. It was to London one looked in establishing a serious career. This was a provincial matter, a colonial survival. It was the sum of similar impulses, in former generations of Irish writers setting themselves up in England, that had left Ireland without a 'real' publisher. The same impulse continues, and still works against the development of an adequate professional publishing industry in Ireland. There is a practical reason, having to do with the small Irish market and the economics of distribution, but difficulties of this kind are soluble. The post-colonial impulse is the deciding consideration: primary publication in England is regarded as the desirable norm by most Irish writers and by the commentators. It is Richard Ellmann's own opinion, dealing with Joyce's manoeuverings with Maunsel over the publication of *Dubliners,* that there would be a 'wider, less provincial audience if some English publisher would take the book ...'.

Later Irish poets followed Yeats, as best they could, in looking for English publishers. They found them, for reasons which are reasonably clear. Padraic Colum's *Wild Earth,* published by Macmillan, consisted mainly of short folk songs, and satisfied the same kind of expectations for Irish poetry as Yeats's early work. James Stephens made his name by 'the exquisite prose of the delightful fairy stories' in *The Crock of Gold*, and generally by his 'sense of fantasy' and 'delicate poetic talent'. Louis MacNeice, from a colonial family in Northern Ireland, and fully at home in Britain, was accepted direct into the English poetry of his time. Patrick Kavanagh, ill at ease at home or abroad, had a publishing history as mixed as Beckett's: his first book, *Ploughman and Other Poems*, was published by Macmillan in 1936; a limited edition of *The Great Hunger* was published by the expiring Cuala Press in 1942, with the commercial edition in *A Soul for Sale* by Macmillan in 1947; subsequent books were published privately by Kavanagh's brother in New York and by Longmans in London, with the *Collected Poems* in New York and by MacGibbon & Kee.

Austin Clarke had two phases in his publishing career. Early poems, decorative and historical, and dramas in decorative Irish settings, were published by Maunsel and, later in the 1920s and 1930s, by Allen and Unwin in London; with a book of collected poems in 1936. The publication of Clarke's dramas — comedies and 'pantomimes' with titles like *The Viscount of Blarney* or *As the Crow Flies* — continued with private first editions and commercial editions from Williams and Norgate in London. But the more difficult later poetry, appearing first in *Night and Morning* in 1938, failed to find an English publisher. This poetry developed in privately published books and found a commercial publisher in Ireland only late in Clarke's career. This was the Dolmen Press.

The Dolmen Press was founded in Dublin in 1951, with an interest primarily in fine printing and design. Many of the Press's early publications were hand-set experimental pamphlets where the literary content mattered little. But from the beginning the Press set itself the object of publishing work by Irish authors and soon found itself dealing with a new Irish poetry. For the next three decades it provided professional primary publication in Ireland for Irish and other poetry and drama, with commentary on Irish and Anglo-Irish literature.

Educational and university publishers, and some Dublin bookshops, had formerly attempted to provide for the local publication of poetry and other work. And there was a nationalist and a religious press. But the Dolmen Press, due partly to its success in publicity and marketing, was the first to publish on a professional basis, initially on a small scale, and to survive. The Press's publications included poetry and translations from the Irish by the new Irish writers of the 1950s, with publications by some of the older established writers, reprints of poetry and drama from the nineteenth and early twentieth centuries — by Allingham and others — and editions of medieval and bardic Irish poetry; all in pursuit of a policy of filling the gaps in Irish publishing. By the mid-1950s the Press had a full list of publications, with an emphasis on poetry. New writers, especially of poetry, were accepted — if they were publishable at all — making publication outside Ireland a matter of choice by the writer. Beginning in the early 1960s the problem of external distribution was solved by a system of co-publication, for individual titles, with commercial publishers in Britain and the United States.

The Press was an expression of individual energy. Liam Miller, the founder, died in 1987 and the Press has not survived. But it has had a continuing effect in a new generation of Irish publishers, so that professional primary publication is now available in Ireland.

From *The Dual Tradition: An Essay on Poetry and Politics in Ireland*, Peppercanister 18 / Carcanet (1995).

II *The Early Years*

Beginning among the particulars. Hiking in the Dublin hills in the late 1940s; encountering a military gentleman who frequented the youth hostels, and visiting him in his top flat in Grafton Street, unaware of risk. Listening to his records of classical music and talking of poetry. Admiring a pamphlet, in proof, of his verse — *Noblesse* — illustrated by himself with peacock on balustrade. To be published soon by a hiker I had yet to meet: Billy Miller.

Outside, a Grafton Street smelling of turf smoke and horse-drawn traffic, and a Dublin of small-scale politics still venomous with memories of civil war. My contemporaries — only recently left school — leaving the country, emigration the only apparent opportunity. Yeats overshadowing anybody's early poetic preoccupations, and all of poetry in English. But Joyce the great Fact, relevant in every experience.

Austin Clarke in Templeogue, silent since 1938 and the publication of *Night and Morning*, except for a priestlike weekly radio programme. Patrick Kavanagh seeming more a comic prop than a poet, in his pose of martyrdom for the Truth; but with a raw power in some early poems and in *The Great Hunger*. Valentin Iremonger published in book form. Anthony Cronin and Pearse Hutchinson, passed through UCD in a recent brilliant generation, being published in magazines. One or two in my own generation making the first move toward commitment.

London the place of significant exile. Austin Clarke had spent a whole generation of his life there. People said that Patrick Kavanagh was there much of the time, because there was 'nothing in Ireland'. London was where books were published. Kavanagh's *A Soul for Sale* had been published by Macmillan. And Valentin Iremonger's *Reservations*. A book by Donagh MacDonagh had been published by Faber & Faber, where T.S. Eliot was Director — a great achievement.

There was a literary scene in Dublin: newspapermen, novelists, poets and playwrights meeting in certain pubs on stated evenings to talk about art and things in general. 'Connoisseurs' conversation', Robert Farren called it. Farren was one of them. He had written poetry and was committed to a concept of Irishness which he had set out in a book called *The Course of Irish Verse*. Irishness involved high moods and had a murmuring quality, as I understood it, with a wavering music of long lines and internal rhyme; and it was Catholic. Farren's book shifted uneasily at the thought of modern poetry. It admitted that there have been violent innovations in modern poetry; and Irish poetry, no less than that of other countries, reflects these changes. The influences of Eliot, Pound and their English juniors have penetrated to Ireland; Hopkins's strong hand has been laid on us as on others; and Chesterton has not quite passed us by.

*

In 1950 I met Liam Miller, no longer Billy. A draftsman in an architect's office, thin and intense, living with his wife Jo and his young family in a cottage in Ringsend. Setting up, letter by letter, and printing on an Adana hand-press broadsides and ballads, decorative cards and exhibition catalogues, and programmes for the production of plays by George Fitzmaurice, J.M. Synge and Lady Gregory; productions often designed and staged by Miller himself.

He had published a book: *Travelling Tinkers*, by Sigerson Clifford. Publication was an undefined occurrence, when the last of the edition was stitched and bound by hand, and a supply — slim and expensive — put in Miller's briefcase to be sold in the Dublin bookshops.

Publication of a first book of verse, Herman Melville has said, is of all human events the least significant. In March of 1952 the Dolmen Press published *The Starlit Eye*, a poem of mine of fifty lines, in separate covers: a book of eight pages with illustrations by the publisher, in a limited edition numbered and signed. It was given a careful welcome in *Poetry Ireland*: '... a debut which kindles one's interest a great deal ... well worth reading'. The Press published another pamphlet of mine in December, *Three Legendary Sonnets,* in an edition of one hundred copies, in various covers, also numbered and signed. And one in March of 1953 — *Per Imaginem* — in a special edition of twenty-five copies, for the marriage of a friend.

*

The association with the Press from its beginning, when it was a kitchen industry, is an experience for which I have always been grateful. I visited the household regularly, impressed always by the fusion of business and family activity, the scene cheerful and intense; writers, artists and professionals meeting in the small room in great numbers. Miller's style and craftsmanship — his commitment to quality in design, material and finish — were unrelenting. And his interests were various, many of them new to me; including the prose and poetry in Old Irish.

I made some translations at his suggestion, using my knowledge of modern School Irish. *Faeth Fiadha — The Deer's Cry: The Breastplate of*

Saint Patrick — 'Faith's trunk armour ... '. An incantation with biblical power, composed by Patrick in Irish to shield him and his monks 'from deadly enemies who were ambushing the clerics'. This gave me a first feeling of the character of the literature in Old Irish. The translation, with designs by Captain Henry Neville Roberts, was issued on Saint Brigid's Day 1954.

In *The Sons of Usnech,* an eighth-century prose tale with passages in verse, I encountered the real Deirdre, and high literature in Irish. A masterpiece of concise and passionate narrative, sobering and exciting at once; a savage and direct story of nobility and love, and treachery so close to the animal as to be almost innocent. Nothing like Deirdre of the Sorrows — in her stage melancholy, with her air of false folk. And an awakening from the Irish language, nationalist and pure in heart, as I had known it until then; with a wish to know more.

In December 1954, a version of *The Deer's Cry,* with illustrations by Louis le Brocquy based on megalithic designs, was printed by the Dolmen Press on a Christmas card 'for the friends of John McGuire'; a combination of elements emphasizing the pagan, and the first indication of Miller's thoughts for an edition of *The Táin.*

The previous month the Press had published *The Ballad of Jane Shore* by Donagh MacDonagh, with a hand-coloured design by Eric Patton, the first part of a new enterprise: The Dolmen Chapbook, 'an illustrated miscellany'. The Chapbook continued irregularly into the 1960s, one of a number of enabling ideas which provided Miller with continuing opportunities for experiment in design. I contributed at his suggestion some translations of Irish triads, with drawings by Pauline Bewick. These were published as Part IV of the Chapbook in 1955. In 1956 an original poem of mine, *Death of a Queen*, illustrated by Bridget Swinton, was published as Part V, and permitted to disappear.

*

In 1956 my first book was published by the Press — *Poems, 1956* — a book of love poems for my wife Eleanor; we had married in December 1955. The book was prepared and published almost without my being aware of the process, with no space between writer and publisher that might have been filled with pose or self-esteem. Unself-conscious publication is an aspect of my relationship with the Press that remained valuable.

It was in a few of these poems that I became sure. With means partly borrowed — some crippling modes, and titles — but with their own matter; some of them surviving, even still, the years of scrutiny and selection. *Poems, 1956*, was a plain and elegant book with all of Miller's excellences: perfection of design, materials and presentation. And in every copy that I could find, years afterward, with the last poem razored out and the title pasted over.

III *The Dolmen Press Limited*

In 1956 Miller gave up his other work and established the Press full time, with myself as a Director — an honorary appointment with no function. From this time onward the Press provided a full range of publishing, including professional publication for poetry for the first time in Ireland.

The effect of this showed quickly in the career of Austin Clarke. Clarke had produced in 1955, after his long silence, a private pamphlet of verse, *Ancient Lights*, from his own Bridge Press in Templeogue. These were bitter and satirical poems of local intensity. They could seem obscure, but there was no mistaking their power. And the Dolmen Press published Clarke's *Too Great a Vine* the next year, showing that *Ancient Lights* was not to remain an isolated achievement. Clarke's subsequent career was startling: a succession of notable Dolmen Press books, in a late flourish of poetry of eccentric ease — an ease of liberation; the eccentricity the effect, in part, of his long artistic silence.

In 1958 my own *Poems, 1956,* were collected with other poems written in my top room in Baggot Street, where I had lived some years on my own and for a while with Eleanor after our marriage; and with new poems written out of County Wexford, where her people came from. I met her family there and, for the first time, another Ireland: provincial, Protestant and long-established; confident and oriented towards England. I wrote a few poems, in growing self-awareness, dealing with this new matter on its own ground, and added these to the love poems.

Another September was a professional-looking book, benefiting again by Miller's skills. Especially by his skill in marketing — by his placing it so that it might be 'chosen' by the Poetry Book Society, overcoming by this certain post-colonial hesitations on the part of Irish booksellers and reviewers, and establishing the Press as a publisher whose books could be accepted with ordinary confidence.

One problem remained, arising from the Press's base in Ireland and the limit this set to the scale of distribution, particularly outside of Ireland. This was overcome by an accidental but, in retrospect, inevitable development. The poet Robin Skelton had visited Dublin in 1960, and mentioned later in Oxford University Press that I might be looking for an English publisher. After an initial misunderstanding, when it was thought I wanted to leave the Dolmen Press, the idea of joint publication emerged, with Dolmen handling Irish distribution and Oxford handling the rest. This set a pattern for a relationship between Dolmen and other publishers. The first outcome was the joint publication of *Downstream* in 1962.

*

In 1965 I was employed still as a civil servant, in the Department of Finance. I had experienced six months of creative freedom in 1963, when I took special leave from the Department to begin work on a translation of *The Táin*. It was necessary for the grant to use it in the United States, and I had divided the time between Boston and San Francisco.

In 1965 I was offered a position at Southern Illinois University at Carbondale, giving one lecture per year, with my time otherwise to myself. Not exactly what I would have chosen. But exactly what the work required. In the next three years I finished *The Táin* and an amount of new poetry, much of the poetry involved with the stresses of the time before the change; stresses one had scarcely been conscious of, they were so thoroughly a part of the nature of things — but, now that one had left, clear for inspection: the troubled intimate relations, in *Wormwood*, 1966;

the bureaucrat out-of-phase — in *Nightwalker*, 1967 — worrying at his situation with images out of Goethe and Astounding Science Fiction; and — in 'Phoenix Park', 1968 — the circuit of summing up and departure.

The Táin, finished the following year, benefited by one of the comforts of the American academic system so that, shortly after leaving Ireland, I was enabled to return: as a Guggenheim Fellow, for a year spent in the peace of Raglan Road and in the assembly of the big Dolmen Press book. The great pagan story saved by the baffled commitment of a Christian scribe — of whom one was at all times aware; the text and Louis le Brocquy's illustrations, and the maps, coming together under Miller's guidance and control; the narrative and drawings balanced between the baleful and the comic, never entirely settling for one or the other; yet with everything totally serious, each of us putting forth his best efforts, Miller exerting maximum pressure with the lightest of touches.

The Route of the Táin

Gene sat on a rock, dangling our map.
The others were gone over the next crest,
further astray. We ourselves, irritated,
were beginning to turn down toward the river
back to the car, the way we should have come.

The Dolmen Press

We should have trusted our book.
After they tried a crossing, and this river too
'rose against them' and bore off
a hundred of their charioteers toward the sea
They had to move along the river Colptha
up to its source.
                        There:
Where the main branch sharpens away gloomily
to a gash in the hill opposite.

then to Bélat Ailiúin
                                    by that pathway
climbing back and forth out of the valley
over to Ravensdale.

Scattering in irritation. Who had set out
so cheerfully to celebrate our book;
cheerfully as we made and remade it
through a waste of hours, content to 'enrich the present
honouring the past', each to his own just function.
Wandering off, ill-sorted,
like any beasts of the field,
one snout honking disconsolate,
another burrowing in its pleasures.

When not far above us a red fox
ran at full stretch out of the bracken
and panted across the hillside toward the next ridge.
Where he vanished — a faint savage sharpness
out of the earth — an inlet of the sea
shone in the distance at the mouth of the valley
beyond Omeath: grey waters crawled with light.

For a heartbeat, in alien certainty,
we exchanged looks. We should have known it by now
— the process, the whole tedious enabling ritual.
Flux brought to fullness; saturated;
the clouding over; dissatisfaction

spreading slowly like an ache;
something reduced shivering suddenly
into meaning along new boundaries;

through a forest,
by a salt-dark shore,
by a standing stone on a dark plain,
by a ford running blood,
and along this gloomy pass, with someone ahead
calling and waving on the crest
against a heaven of dismantling cloud,
transfixed by the same figure (stopped, pointing)
on the rampart at Cruachan, where it began.

The morning sunlight pouring on us all
as we scattered over the mounds
disputing over useless old books,
assembled in cheerful speculation
around a prone block, *Miosgán Medba*
— Queen Medb's *turd* ...? And rattled our maps,
joking together in growing illness
or age or fat. Before us
the route of the Táin, over men's dust,
toward these hills that seemed to grow
darker as we drove nearer.

(1971)

IV *Peppercanister and the Dolmen Press*

Peppercanister was established in 1972 as a small publishing enterprise, issuing occasional special items from our home in Dublin, across the Grand Canal from St Stephen's Church, known locally as 'The Peppercanister'.

The idea originated with *Butcher's Dozen,* written in April 1972 in response to the Widgery Report on the 'Bloody Sunday' shootings in Derry. The poem was finished quickly and issued as a simple pamphlet at ten pence a copy; cheapness and coarseness were part of the effect, as with a ballad sheet. The Dolmen Press was not involved with *Butcher's Dozen,* but Liam Miller was personally interested and helped with practical suggestions.

A Selected Life was issued as a commemorative elegy for Seán Ó Riada, with *Butcher's Dozen* as a precedent but using better materials, and designed by Liam Miller for the serious occasion. *Vertical Man* was issued a year later as a sequel in the same format. The fourth title, *The Good Fight,* was issued as a small public pamphlet with some of the character of *Butcher's Dozen.*

It seemed that Peppercanister was developing as a means of dealing with occasional public items. But the next titles were different, in content and purpose. *One* and *A Technical Supplement* were closer to book-length and contained sequences of a more private poetry. Used in this way, for sequences and short collections, Peppercanister became an alternative to the publication of poetry in literary journals. Later Peppercanister sequences and short collections were *Song of the Night and Other Poems, Songs of the Psyche, Personal Places, Poems from Centre City,* and *Madonna.*

The idea proved useful also for the separate publication of long poems: *The Messenger, Her Vertical Smile, Out of Ireland,* and *St. Catherine's Clock*; and of two satirical poems: *One Fond Embrace,* and *Open Court*.

Most of the Peppercanister titles were issued with special editions, on handmade paper, boxed, and with full leather bindings. I had admired Liam Miller's commitment to quality in materials and design, and for a while this was confused with the Peppercanister idea. But the production and distribution of special editions is a special matter, and Peppercanister as it has developed is useful above all as a form of interim publication, providing an extra draft of the text, in book form, before final publication.

From the preface to *Peppercanister 1972–1997: Twenty-five Years of Poetry,* compiled by Stephen Enniss (Emory University Archives and Libraries Series, No. 3, 1997).

v *Endings*

The business affairs of the Dolmen Press, including the basis for the occasional royalties on my own books, were never revealed to me. I was content with this in the early years of the Press, in the atmosphere of enthusiasm and goodwill and in the belief that all funds were needed by the Press. The books, embodying Liam Miller's commitment and genius, were all that I required. I knew that it was a privilege to have his abilities and energies always available for my work, with our understandings shared and the work always primary. For many years I remained content with this arrangement. But as the Press continued to survive, a wider family element entered the business. The atmosphere changed, while the air of monetary mystery remained, and on the 22 August 1986 I wrote resigning my Directorship. The scene at the closing down of the Press in 1989, after Miller's death, was painful: the debtors hurt and blaming; his daughter in an impossible position, exposed finally to their questions.

*

Thomas Kinsella

At the graveside: 19 May 1987

I am grieved that this occasion has come. But, since it has, I am honoured to have this chance to say something of what I feel — and I know that others feel — about Liam Miller.

There is no way to make a sufficient short statement about him. I have known him for most of a lifetime, as a man of imagination, skill and practical sense; of faith and national feeling; of energy and patience, and great generosity and kindness. I knew him since I was a young man, and had discovered that there was something I wanted to do as best I could. And I soon knew that I was lucky to have met Liam Miller, with his certainty and dedication. I have spent the years since then in admiration of him and his achievements; as he established real publishing in Ireland, so that the idea of necessary publication elsewhere disappeared; as he contributed to three generations of Irish poetry — restoring dignity to the career of Austin Clarke; giving a professional base to the new poetry of the 1950s and 1960s; and providing the precedent for the new generation of Irish publishing. I have admired the liberality and the inspired directness of his design, as he solved one major problem after another: the intimate but dignified presentation of modern poetry; the presentation of an ancient text like the *Táin Bó Cuailgne,* with the inspired commissioning and use of illustrations; his design of the new Missal — practical, elegant and devout; and one of his last and most successful books, the book on Irish stamps, full of vigour and personal enthusiasm, like his early and equally successful books on Yeats's poetic drama — his powers working to the full, regardless of the apparent grandeur or modesty of the aim. And I have admired his achievements as they accumulated into an overall personal achievement, based on a concern for the Irish tradition in all its manifestations. I admired him most, perhaps, in his last illness, as he found ease in his work still, designing works that would never appear, his ideas as sharp as ever in the service of the same purpose.

His family and friends knew his humanity face to face. His country knows it. And it is known internationally as he showed it in his work, with scope and inclusiveness as well as with minute care, all amounting to a notable and successful life's work. He has left his mark on many things and set many things moving. And he has left us great example.